Ruth and Naomi

Ruth and Naomi

Ellen van Wolde

SCM PRESS LTD

Translated by John Bowden from the Dutch *Ruth en Naömi, twee vreemdgangers*, published 1993 by Uitgeverij Ten Have, b.v., Baarn, with revisions by the author, 1997.

0 334 02694 6

First published 1997 by
SCM Press Ltd
9–17 St Albans Place London N1 0NX

Typeset by Regent Typesetting, London
and printed in Great Britain by
Biddles Ltd, Guildford and King's Lynn

Contents

Through Boaz's eyes   37

Through Ruth's eyes   49

Ruth 3: Midnight   64

Through Naomi's eyes   66

Through Ruth's eyes   75

viii

No hay caminos
hay que caminar

There is no way
to go alone

Inscription in a monastery in Toledo

Introduction

Ruth as a story of headscarves

A stream of headscarves goes through history. We sometimes see them as the background to television pictures of politicians who enjoy posing for the camera, shaking hands and drawing crowds. The headscarves do not pose. Bent over against the cold or the heat, they tear at one's heart as they stand mourning by the graves of their dead husbands or slaughtered sons. They fight over scarce pieces of bread or look for water in order to keep their children and grandchildren alive. They go away from their destroyed homes, fleeing the violence of war. Who keeps history going, one asks, the politicians or these women? Survival evidently happens under cover.

The headscarves are a byway of history. The biblical book of Ruth takes place on such a byway. Two migrant women, Naomi and Ruth, are widows and have great difficulty in surviving. After much sorrow and inventiveness they succeed. Eventually they even have a child who is to become the ancestor of King David. However, the genealogy at the end of the book has only included the names of the fathers and so this byway is brought back to the main road.

The book of Ruth is still closed. Soon we shall be taken on a journey though a world which is not ours, and we shall come up against the strange world of foreigners: they are like us, and remain different from us. We can develop an eye for them, but their eyes never coincide with ours. And our effort at understanding is specifically directed towards achieving their perspective: we want to see what they see and feel what they feel. Yet the moment that we think that we have been successful here, we often discover that our perspective does not coincide with theirs but theirs with ours; and so usually we have reduced the other to ourselves again. It's like the story of the rabbi who all his life has made an effort to be humble. After a long life of practising this he thinks, 'Now at last I've become humble. I'm as humble as anyone can be. I'm a champion of humility.' And immediately he realizes, 'I have to begin all over again.'

Ruth is not just an illegal alien in Bethlehem but also a woman, in a society in which women only become someone as 'wife of', 'daughter of', 'sister of'. So when all these men – the husband, the father or the brother – disappear, such a woman completely ceases to exist. Even to be a daughter-in-law, as Ruth is, is not a real alternative. Certainly not if the mother-in-law, who in her turn derives her identity only from her husband and her sons, no longer has either husband or sons. It is difficult to derive your identity from someone who herself has no identity. All that is left is illegal work, dirty and heavy work to stay alive. In her case it is gleaning ears of grain, standing all day bent over and working hard for a handful of grains of wheat or barley. How can any one doing that become visible, one might wonder? Sometimes an invisible someone encounters good people. Sometimes someone finds a story-teller who thinks it important to make the invisible visible, and sometimes as a reader one becomes part of a tradition which believes in a God who has a weakness for headscarves.

Seeing and reading

Even then the question remains: how does one as a reader get something into one's head and framework of thought? Is it possible for a time to see with the eyes of someone else, even if that someone is a character in a story, or a narrator? Precisely because it is difficult to adapt one's own way of looking, here I have opted for a systematic approach. My purpose is to offer present-day readers some help in reading a biblical text methodically and seeing different facets of the book of Ruth. The approach is laid out at the back of the book in the form of a guide to reading. This guide indicates the perspectives, the lines and the elements that the text offers the reader. We see what Naomi or Ruth sees, or we adopt the perspective of the narrator who orders everything in terms of his view and presents it to the reader. Time and again different perspectives and lines will become visible in the text, depending on the perspective you as reader choose, on the cross-section you make, the elements you accept. Thus making visible means putting a searchlight on the text in order to light up elements of it. In reading, even systematic reading, seldom, if ever, is everything seen. Some facets become visible, and together these form a kind of facet-eye. Thus we gradually develop an eye which is our own eye, and in it the views of other people and their perspectives are included. To emphasize this, in this book I shall sometimes put passages, passages in which we look through the eyes of a character in the first person, in italics. That may perhaps also bring out the different perspectives from which one can look at reality and at the text.

A miniature

The story of Ruth is very short. It's like a mediaeval miniature. You marvel at a miniature more and more, the longer you look at it through a magnifying glass. So you will also be caught up in Ruth, certainly if you read it in the Hebrew. The language has a dominant presence; words keep recurring, lines are spun, and a tower of images reaches up to heaven. It is difficult to translate such a text. Either the translation is very faithful to the text but stiff and cold, in which case there is no question of attraction or charm. Or the translation is more poetical in English, with the consequence that it is further from the Hebrew. I have opted for a literal translation of Ruth, chapter by chapter, and in it to indicate the Hebrew sentence- or phrase-construction, making clear by the lay-out of the text when a character offers the information (indentation) or when it is provided by the narrator (no indentation); at the same time I wanted to achieve a readable text.

The book of Ruth is not just a story; you could also call it a short play. It consists of four acts, which are written out in four chapters. If you were watching a stage performance, I think that it would last about half an hour. If you read the book straight through, it will take even less. Yet here is a book of 160 pages about such a short story. Unimaginable? Yes. But it takes time to create connections in language and to bring out meanings which give some indication of another life and offer the possibility of getting into someone else's skin.

Ruth 1: The Journey

1a In the days when the judges gave leadership
there was a famine in the land.

1b So a man went from Bethlehem in Judah
to live as an emigrant in the country of Moab,
he, his wife and his two sons.

2a The name of the man was Elimelek,
the name of his wife was Naomi
and the names of his two sons were Mahlon and Chilion.
They were Ephrathites from Bethlehem in Judah.

2b When they came to the country of Moab
they settled there.

3a Then Elimelek, the husband of Naomi, died.

3b She was left, she and her two sons.

4a These took Moabite wives.
The name of the one was Orpah,
the name of the second was Ruth,

4b and they lived there about ten years.

5a Then these two, Mahlon and Chilion, also died.

5b The wife was left, without her two children and her husband.

6a She arose, she and her daughters-in-law,
and returned from the country of Moab,

6b for she had heard in the fields in Moab
that YHWH had visited his people to give them bread.

7a Thereupon she set out from the place
where she had lived,
and her two daughters-in-law with her.

7b They went on the way to return to the land of Judah.

8a But Naomi said to her two daughters-in-law:
'Go!
Return, a woman to the house of her mother!

8b May YHWH show goodness to you,
as you have shown it to the dead and to me.

9a May YHWH grant you
that you find rest, a woman in the house of her husband.'

9b   When she kissed them farewell,
        they raised their voices
        and burst into tears.
10a   They said to her,
10b   'We want to return with you to your people.'
10   Naomi said:
        'Turn back, my daughters!
        Why should you go with me?
11b   Do I still have sons in my womb
        who can become your husbands?
12a   Turn back, my daughters!
        Go!
        For I am too old to have a husband.
12b   Even if I said
        "There is still hope for me,"
        even if I belonged to a man tonight,
        and actually bore sons,
13a   would you wait
        till they grew up?
        Would you withhold yourselves so long
        from belonging to a man?
13b   No, my daughters!
        It is much more bitter for me than for you,
        YHWH's own hand has struck me.'
14a   They raised their voices,
        and burst into tears again.
14b   Then Orpah kissed her mother-in-law farewell,
        but Ruth clung to her.
15a   She said,
        'See,
        your sister-in-law is going back to her people and her God.
15b   Go back, follow your sister-in-law.'
16a   But Ruth said,
        'Do not press me
        to abandon you,
        to go back from following you,
        Where you go
        I shall go.
        Where you spend the night,
        I shall spend the night.
        Your people is my people,
        your God is my God.

17a   Where you die
      I shall die,
      and there shall I be buried.

17b   Thus may YHWH do to me
      and thus may he continue to do.
      Nothing but death will separate me from you.'

18a   She saw
      that she was determined
      to go with her.

18b   And she refrained from
      speaking to her.

19a   The two of them went on
      until they got to Bethlehem.

19b   And it happened
      when they came into Bethlehem
      that the whole town buzzed with excitement over them.
      They said,
        'Is this really Naomi?'

20a   But she told them,
        'Do not call me Naomi (Lovely),

20b   call me Mara (Bitter),
      for the Almighty has made me very bitter.

21a   I went away full,
      and YHWH has made me return empty.

21b   Why do you call me Naomi?
      YHWH has testified against me,
      the Almighty has done evil to me.'

22a   So Naomi returned and Ruth the Moabitess her daughter-in-law
      with her,
      who returned from the country of Moab.

22b   They arrived in Bethlehem at the beginning of the barley
      harvest.

Through the eye of the needle

There is a famine. Even in Bethlehem, the house (*bet*) of bread (*lehem*), there is no longer anything to eat. So a man goes away from Bethlehem in Judah with his family. His name is Elimelek, 'my God is king'. The situation is serious: the one whose God is king is fleeing from the house of bread because of famine. He goes away to a land where other Gods are king and where there is enough to eat. In that land, Moab, live people who speak another language, with other customs and another religion. The man and his family go towards an uncertain future. The need must have been very great for them to have been prepared to take such a risk. They go there as migrants, as resident aliens. At that time, being a migrant was a status with virtually no protection, midway between the full rights of the indigenous population and the lack of rights of the slave. Such an alien could not buy land and cultivate a property like the native population, but could enter the service of indigenous employers, usually landowners, and thus earn his living.

The narrator tells his story from the perspective of Elimelek, as the possessive pronouns show. The woman is twice called 'his' wife and the sons 'his' sons. The name of Elimelek's wife is Naomi, which means 'pleasant' or 'lovely'. Those of the sons are less clear. The names Mahlon and Chilion rhyme and have the same rhythm of two syllables. They also always appear together. In short, they form an indissoluble pair like Bill and Ben or Wallace and Grommit. Here the text puts great emphasis on the number two: 'the man and his *two* sons went away', 'the names of his *two* sons were', 'she and her *two* sons remained after Elimelek's death', 'then the *two* also died', and 'the woman was robbed of her *two* children'. We now certainly know that there were two of them.

These two sons marry two women from Moab. However, the word 'marry' does not appear here, nor indeed does it occur anywhere in the Hebrew Bible. Every time men 'take' a wife, our Bible translations render this 'marry'. Marriage and marrying are much later inventions, which for convenience are projected back on these texts. That does not mean that 'take a wife' or 'go into a wife' does not at the same time indicate the start of a lasting relationship between man and woman. But it is not an equal relationship for the two of them. The woman is tied to the man, but the man is not exclusively tied to the woman; he can take another wife. It is evident from many biblical texts that the procreation of children is central to any man–woman relationship. So the texts mention taking, becoming pregnant and giving birth in the same breath (see also Ruth 4.13). If you didn't know better, you would think that all this took place in a couple of hours. Problems arise when the woman does not become pregnant, but is infertile. Men were never infertile at that time.

So Elimelek's sons take foreign wives, one called Orpah and the other Ruth. We are not told who marries whom. Because Mahlon and Chilion, and Orpah and Ruth, always appear in this order, one might think that Mahlon married Orpah and Chilion Ruth. This idea can even be maintained up to the end of the book of Ruth: up to 4.9,10, to be precise. There Chilion and Mahlon are mentioned in reverse order, and then it proves that Ruth was the wife of Mahlon. It is amazing that the reader has to wait to the end of the book to discover that Ruth was 'married' to Mahlon. Perhaps that doesn't really matter. The only thing that counts is that the brothers from Judah both take Moabite women as wives.

The two Moabite women at first only appear together, just like the brothers. The meaning of the names Orpah and Ruth is unknown. The name Orpah is sometimes explained from the word '*orep*, neck. Because she is the one who later turns her back on Naomi, her name has something to do with neck. Ruth's name has no demonstrable meaning. At the same time, it is the only name in this story which consists only of one syllable, which is very rare in the Bible. Its brevity and pronunciation make the name a striking one. Nor does this name Ruth appear elsewhere in the Hebrew Bible, as the name of anyone else. It is striking that the main character in the book, after whom the book is even named, does not have a name with any meaning that we can explain, while others, like Elimelek and Naomi, do have well-known names. But of course they also come from Judah. Probably here the names of these foreign women do not add anything. Ruth's name gives no indication of how we can look at her. We see her only as a foreigner, as the people of Judah see her, and as we often see Muslim or Pakistani women. We see only the headscarf, with a spherical shape beneath it; the outside and outsider's clothing limit our perception.

So at the beginning of the book of Ruth we are looking at the world with a family from Bethlehem. They are called 'Ephrathites'. Evidently that is a well-known term for the inhabitants of Judah. We know only that Ephrath or Ephratha occurs in Genesis 35.19: 'Rachel was buried on the way to

Ephrath(a) (that is, Bethlehem).' That can mean that Ephrath(a)
is the old name for Bethlehem and that 'Ephrathites' denotes the
oldest indigenous families of Bethlehem. Members of an old and
distinguished Bethlehem family have to flee because of a famine
and emigrate to Moab. It is as if members of the Rockefeller
family had to flee and emigrate

Through Naomi's eyes

Naomi gets her own eyes

As readers, we look with the eyes of the people from Judah,
above all Elimelek. When he suddenly dies, the perspective
immediately shifts to Naomi: 'Then Elimelek, the husband of
Naomi, died' (1.3). A verse earlier Naomi was still called
Elimelek's wife; now he is 'Naomi's husband'. We do not know
why or of what he died; simply that Naomi is left, 'she and her
two sons'. The story pauses only briefly over the two sons. Then
in v.5 there follows an almost identical description to that in
v.3: 'Then these two also died. The wife was left, without her
two children and her husband.' Whoever saw a family die out
so tersely? Did the sons die together as a result of a disaster, or
did one die soon after the other? There is no point in asking
questions here, since the attention of the narrator is focussed on
nothing, or rather no one, but Naomi. He shows how in two
stages she changes from being the 'wife of' and 'mother of' to
'the woman without'. Naomi has lost all that can normally give
one identity. She no longer has a face, yet the readers get the
opportunity to look through her eyes.

Moving from the outside inwards, through Naomi's actions,
perceptions and words, we get a glimpse of her world. We
experience her outside world through what she does or wants to
do, namely to 'return'. She thinks only of one thing, and that is
to go back. She produces variations on that in every key: she
wants to return, turn back, go back, and really returns. Finally
the narrator sums this all up in 1.22: 'Naomi, who returned
from the land of Moab'. This becomes as it were her title: she is
'the one who returned'. We read what she *hears* in 1.6b: 'she
had heard in the fields in Moab that YHWH had visited his people
to give them bread'. In v.1 the narrator had simply mentioned

the bare fact of the famine, without any suggestion that God was behind it. Now Naomi assumes that YHWH is the one who gives bread. In her view, wasn't YHWH then also the one who had withheld bread from his people during the famine? That isn't clear, but seems to be the case. Naomi concludes from what she has heard that YHWH has been involved. That is her 'view', or rather her 'way of hearing' (unfortunately there is no word in English for 'seeing through the ears': perspective, view, vision are all visual categories). Naomi evidently assumes that in reality all events are a consequence of YHWH's activity. Another striking feature of this 'way of hearing' is that Naomi thinks that YHWH had visited 'his' people and not 'her' people. In her understanding, YHWH has distanced himself from her; she no longer belongs to his people.

The narrator again lets us look with Naomi, in 1.18: 'Naomi *saw* that Ruth was determined to go with her.' Naomi wants to go back to Judah; she kisses her daughters-in-law farewell and says that they must stay in Moab. They protest, but Naomi is firm. Only when she sees that Ruth cannot be dissuaded from going with her does she drop her opposition. It is not said that she is madly happy that Ruth is going with her. She does not radiate happiness but resignation; she is not relieved but accepts with a shrug of her shoulders. A little phrase like 'she saw that she was determined' doesn't seem to have much meaning, but that isn't the case. We get a disconcerting glimpse into what Naomi is feeling: Ruth has just laid open her soul to Naomi, and all that Naomi says is . . . nothing. She is silent and remains silent. They both go on their way together, but there doesn't seem to be any 'togetherness' about it. Naomi goes, and Ruth goes with her. Naomi is bitter and doesn't see the positive aspect of Ruth's choice. Perhaps she doesn't want Ruth to be going with her and finds Ruth an encumbrance. Certainly any initiative to go with Naomi comes from Ruth and not from Naomi.

Naomi as the complaining mother-in-law

If we are really to see what Naomi sees and feel what she feels, we can do so by sharing her view through what she says. And that isn't too difficult, since Naomi says a lot, as is clear from the indented parts of the text in the translation. Naomi speaks four times at greater or lesser length. In 1.8–9 she bursts out against her daughters-in-law for the first time, 'Go away and return to your own homes.' She is intent on their return. Only the movement that she wants her daughters-in-law to make is in precisely the opposite direction to the one in which she herself wants to go. Her daughters-in-law (and she lumps Ruth and Orpah together) are Moabite women and do not belong in Judah. They have to go back to their own home. Naomi says, 'Go! Return, a woman to the house of her mother!' Her use of the phrase 'a woman' and the personal pronoun 'her' have dismissive connotations. Nowhere in this chapter or in later chapters of the book of Ruth does Naomi recognize that things must also be hard for Orpah and Ruth. They, too, have lost their spouses, and no longer have husband or children. They have not even ever had children. But Naomi sees things differently, as emerges from what she goes on to say in 1.8–9.

Naomi follows up her call for her daughters to go back with two wishes, which freely translated mean, 'May YHWH do good to you as you have done good to me', and 'May YHWH let you find rest.' These are positive wishes, from which it emerges that she is not just sending her daughters-in-law away, but is also wishing them the best. She wishes them rest, 'a woman in the house of her husband'. The word-play in 'a woman in the house of her husband' is immediately evident. Naomi distances herself from her daughters-in-law without rebuke or malice. On the contrary, she hopes that things will go well with them in the future. They have done good to her and to the dead in the past. But she now distances herself from them and tells them to go back. Unlike her own return, the aim of their return is for them to marry again and find rest in the home of the husband who pleases them. She no longer expects that for herself. Thus we can also hear an implicit complaint in what she says. In the background to 'May YHWH show goodness to you and give you rest in the house of a husband,' we hear, 'YHWH has not done good to me; I have no husband and I shall never find rest.' She does not rebuke her daughters, but rebukes YHWH all the more. Here this complaint still remains implicit, but gradually becomes stronger.

Naomi's picture of God glimmers through all this. As had previously emerged from her perception ('she had heard that YHWH had given bread'), she sees a direct relationship between God's action and events in the world. She wishes for Ruth and Orpah that all the good things that they have done will be reflected in good things which YHWH will do to them. Naomi presupposes and wishes a balance between human action and that of YHWH. YHWH's goodness must correspond to human goodness. That is why she is so disappointed, because YHWH has shown no goodness to her.

The second time that Naomi speaks, this becomes even clearer. Now we really get a good picture of what Naomi is feeling. The first thing that she says is, 'Turn back, why should you go with me? You have nothing more to expect of me. Return and go back' (1.11–13). As if Ruth and Orpah were only going with her to get something in return! Is Naomi revealing her own train of thought here? She then shows her disillusionment: even if she were to sleep with a man that same night and bear sons, her daughters-in-law could not wait until they were old enough to marry them. Once again, Naomi is presupposing that her daughters-in-law are going with her only to get what they got from her previously, a husband. And then comes the complaint from the depths of her heart: 'No, my daughters, it is much more bitter for me than for you, YHWH's own hand has struck me' (1.13b). That's the cause of everything: YHWH has given Naomi short measure. She doesn't know why; she thinks that she hasn't deserved it. 'It's all right for you, daughters-in-law, you can build a new future. I can't.' Once again, she doesn't understand the difficult position of her daughters-in-law, who have also lost their husbands. She has met with much greater sorrow. Really she is immersed only in herself, as can immediately be seen from the use of the first person. She is speaking to her daughters-in-law, but uses the little word 'I' five times in three verses, and 'my' three times. She isn't blaming her daughters-in-law, but loading them with guilt feelings. 'Leave me alone, since I have no future.' But when they then go away she feels abandoned even more. You could call this a subtle ploy, were it not played out with so much passion. It seems to be the classical stereotype of the mother-in-law's role. Nothing is ever right. Her daughters-in-law must go away, since no one will want her. Her daughters-in-law mustn't go away, since then she will be all alone in the world.

Thereupon Orpah resolves to go away. Ruth feels so moved by Naomi's difficult situation that she stays with her, and in return gets anything but gratitude. What was the old saying, 'Ingratitude is the world's reward'? The soft-hearted daughter(-in-law) who is (too) sensitive incurs the most criticism. 'Do what your sister-in-law has done. She at least understood. She is at least doing something. You never do anything. Go back where you came from' (1.15). It's fine to have such a loving mother-in-law.

The fourth and last time that Naomi speaks is the most impressive complaint. When the women in Bethlehem ask, 'Is that Naomi?', she replies angrily, 'Don't call me Naomi, call me Mara.' She distances herself from her last fragment of identity, her name, and exchanges this for a definitive bitterness. We can feel a crescendo in the language: 'The Almighty has made me very bitter. I went away full, and YHWH has made me return empty.' The accusation against YHWH couldn't be harsher. Nor is it completely true. Naomi was not full when she went away. She certainly still had her husband and children, but her stomach was empty because there was a famine, and therefore she and her family had to flee. But memory makes the past better and more attractive by comparison with such a fearful present. Her bitterness has made Naomi blind. She no longer sees that she was not full when she went away, far less that she is not empty now that she is returning. Certainly, her husband and children have died, but Ruth has come with her. So she is not completely empty and alone. Again it is striking how fixated Naomi is upon herself. She uses the word 'me' seven times in two verses and 'I' once. It's almost offensive: 'Don't call me, call me, made me bitter, I went away, made me return, call me, testified against me, brought misery upon me.' Every clause is wholly focussed on the first person: 'I, Naomi, have suffered; injustice has been done to me.'

Naomi directs her accusation against YHWH. YHWH has appeared against her as witness in a heavenly court. She is facing him powerless on earth. But whether one likes it or not,

YHWH is stronger than she is. He is even the strongest of all, the Almighty, who in his omnipotence has poured out this misery on her. Nothing happens without a cause. Things are going badly for her, so YHWH, the Almighty God, must be behind them. She is dishonoured, insulted and deeply disappointed in life and in YHWH.

Naomi's hopeless gaze

People who have had bad experiences and have survived a war and its atrocities often put up shutters on the world. Imagine that someone has just fled the atrocities of war in Rwanda and Zaire. Every night she experiences the rapes and torture anew. Every day she still feels the loss of her husband and two children. Through the Red Cross she is now free and by chance has come to the Britain. Her head is still full of the recent past. Will she look around her? At what? At the full shops, the busy cities or the interesting politics? At other people, even if these are fellow-refugees, each with his or her own suffering? No, these cannot hold her attention. She is too full of her own suffering and has enough to cope with inside herself.

Naomi is like such a woman. Her bitterness is simply one side of her; the hopelessness of her situation is the other. If we look at this side of her, we see how strong Naomi has become. First she was far away from the land of her birth and her own family, in a strange land. Then her husband died; her life became even more difficult, but she rolled up her sleeves and got down to it. She still had her children to look after. And life went on. It was difficult, but things worked out. Until both her children also died. Now she has been robbed of all that was dear to her. She is disillusioned. Life no longer goes on. She goes back to where she came from, though she expects nothing more from it. She has given up long ago. For whom is she to go on being strong?

The moment she arrives in Bethlehem, she experiences everything all over again. She recalls how she went away. Her husband and her sons were still alive. The future didn't seem a rosy one then, but now everything looks pitch dark. And then the 'reception committee' still calls her 'lovely'. 'I'm no longer lovely. I've nothing more in me. I feel empty. Finished. I can't take any more. All those questions about how and why. I just can't cope, I just can't cope. It's too much.' The way in which Naomi reacts is understandable and one can sympathize with it. In her position one would probably do the same. It's rather like Job's situation, except that he still had his wife. Because the narrator describes everything in a matter of fact way, he speaks to us as readers and we sympathize with Naomi. Everything has gone wrong for her.

From the moment that Naomi herself opens her mouth, however, the reader gets increasingly irritated. She has no time for anyone else, for what has happened to her daughters-in-law, for the rest of the world. Certainly in what she says she has become an old bore, and thus causes offence. Her bitterness is absolutely clear. She has no eye for anyone else. So the first chapter of Ruth requires the reader to have a twofold attitude towards Naomi, of sympathy and antipathy at the same time.

In Naomi's own words

I wouldn't wish my life on anyone. At first all seemed to go well. I had a dear father and mother; above all I often think back to my mother. I married very young. My husband, Elimelek, planned the best for me. We soon had two children, two sons. What more could one want? We were happy, but the times were against us. A famine broke out, the worst in human memory. At first only the poor fled from Bethlehem. My husband, from an old impoverished branch of a prominent family in Bethlehem, eventually couldn't find any work either. Only skimpy tufts of grass were left in the fields; wheat no longer grew. We went away; we had to. It was difficult. Saying good-bye was unbearable, the journey itself terribly exhausting, above all because our younger son got sick on the journey. We had to carry him almost all the way. We had heard that work was still to be had in richer Moab. Fortunately they let us in, and my husband found work. We didn't have much contact with the other people; these Moabites have such strange customs. Moreover they're unbelievers, and one mustn't have dealings with them. At first it wasn't easy. Survival was our only concern. We worked fifteen hours a day. But we made it. Thank YHWH.

Suddenly, like a sledgehammer, the hand of YHWH *struck me. First my husband died, quite unexpectedly. Then later my dear children, Mahlon and Chilion, died, in a matter of days. They were still so young; they had no children although they had already been married for ten years. Since then my hope has vanished; I have no future. Without children and grandchildren there is no way ahead for me. What am I to do? If only I were dead! I'm too old to begin a new life. I'm alone in the world. Orpah and Ruth, my two daughters-in-law, are both good women, but they haven't given me grandchildren. Moreover they still have futures. How old will they be? Twenty-five or twenty-six. They can still marry again and have children. But they won't be my grandchildren. I myself am already past forty. I shan't be able to marry again; who will want such an old person? What can the future bring me? Nothing.*

I even thought of putting an end to my life, but that goes against my feelings and my faith. Then I began to think: what courses are still open to me? I can remain here with my two daughters-in-law or I can go home. My parents' house went a long time ago, so going home means above all going to the old house in Bethlehem where my husband and I last lived. That won't be a new future, without husband or children. Another possibility is to remain here in Moab, but I've never felt at home here with all these strange people around me.

No, I'm going back. As quickly as possible. Oh yes, these Moabite wives want to go with me. I can just see myself arriving with them in Bethlehem, I'm so ashamed. They're good women; they've always been good to me and looked after my sons, but they needn't come. Judah is different. Bethlehem is different. They don't believe in YHWH. *Besides, my own faith has been sorely tried. I've not noticed many of the things that I learned in my youth, that* YHWH *is just and rewards people for their good behaviour. My experiences have been pretty bad. Surely it's not fair that all this should have happened to me?*

Through Ruth's eyes

Ruth gets her own eyes

At the beginning of the book Ruth has no eyes of her own. She is simply one of a pair: first of the 'two foreign wives' and later of the 'two daughters-in-law'. Ruth is introduced as the second of the Moabite women, since in v.4 we read literally, 'the name of the one was Orpah, the name of the second was Ruth'. This is a somewhat unusual way of putting it. One would have expected either 'the one and the other' or 'the first and the second'; 'the one and the second' is somewhat strange. When we remember that at the end of the book it proves that Ruth was married to Mahlon, the oldest son, we have to conclude that here Ruth is deliberately put in second place.

After the deaths of their husbands, the two Moabite women are not called widows but 'her (two) daughters-in-law'; in other words they are named in relation to their mother-in-law. The verb-forms in these verses make that very clear: 'she arose, she and her two daughters-in-law', 'she set out from the place where she had lived and her two daughters-in-law with her'. Everything turns on Naomi, whereas the daughters-in-law are somewhat left dangling, both for the narrator and for Naomi herself. Naomi would really rather that they went away.

Thus introduced as a pair, they also appear together when saying farewell. After Naomi has kissed them good-bye, as one woman they raise their voices and burst into tears, saying, 'We want to return with you to your people'. However, Naomi insists once again and even more strongly that they should go home. When they then again raise their voice as one woman and cry loudly, Orpah takes a personal decision and kisses her mother-in-law good-bye. For the first time here we have 'her mother-in-law'. It is as if Orpah now for the first time has her own perspective, as the possessive pronoun 'her' shows. Only on going away has Orpah become an independent person, and ceased to be more or less a daughter-in-law. Ruth doesn't want to say good-bye to Naomi and is left alone as a daughter-in-law.

Ruth puts her arms around Naomi as a sign that she is not going away. And how does Naomi react? She says, 'Look, your sister-in-law is going back to her people and her God. Go back, follow her' (1.15). She so to speak pushes Ruth away. Nevertheless, there is something strange in the personal pronouns which Naomi uses: 'your' sister-in-law, 'her' people and 'her' God. Naomi makes a distinction between Orpah and Ruth, something that she has not done before. Now that Orpah has said good-bye and Ruth has not, Naomi has begun to see a difference between the two. For the first (and last) time she calls Orpah 'your sister-in-law' in talking to Ruth, and for the first time approaches Orpah and Ruth in their relation to each other, and not in relation to herself. And at the same time she recognizes the difference between the two of them: Orpah's people is not Ruth's people and Orpah's God is not Ruth's God. Naomi is right in her feeling, since Ruth will say just the same thing.

From v.14b on, Ruth is born as an independent subject, and no longer half of a pair. The narrator uses the word 'two' once again, but then it is for Naomi and Ruth as they go together towards Bethlehem (1.19). Thus the number 'two' clearly indicates a development within Chapter 1: from two sons, to two daughters-in-law, to Ruth and her mother-in-law, or, better, to Naomi and her daughter-in-law. The book will continue with this last pair. As readers, in Chapter 1 we once have an opportunity to look through Ruth's eyes, and what Ruth herself has to say is in direct speech.

Ruth's deliberate choice

Naomi may be rather tiresome, but in most books and children's Bibles Ruth is depicted as a humble and modest woman, who sacrifices herself for her mother-in-law. She remains in the background and does not push herself forward. She does what she has to do without a fuss, and accepts her lowly position. She is content with it. She doesn't need anything higher, anything more. So Ruth has become a model which churches are fond of offering to their believers, above all of course women. Make yourself a cipher, be lowly and obedient, and then you will be a good believer.

However, this humble and obedient picture of Ruth does not fit the text of the book of Ruth. We find traces to the contrary in every chapter. Here in Chapter 1 it is immediately clear that

Ruth is anything but obedient. She goes against Naomi's wish, explicitly stated three times, that she should go away and return to her family in Moab. What precisely does she say in verses 16 and 17? She begins, 'Do not press me to abandon you or to go back from following you.' Ruth, an obedient woman? Not at all. She wants to go her own way and **not** to be forced by Naomi. So she sets her own wishes over against Naomi's wish. She proves to have a will of her own, and expresses it in a thoughtful way. Naomi had said, 'Go back, follow your sister-in-law' (1.15). Now Ruth uses precisely the same words 'go back', 'follow', and 'you', but in the opposite sense, when she says, 'Do not prevent me from going back with you.' Ruth identifies going back to Moab with turning her back on Naomi. She is aware of the choice and also puts it into words: it is the choice between the Orpah–Ruth relationship and the Naomi–Ruth relationship, and above all between Orpah's people and Naomi's people. And on the basis of this awareness she makes her own choice against Naomi's will. Thus Ruth is certainly not docile or obedient: 'Don't force me, I shall make up my own mind' could be her motto.

Ruth behaves in precisely the opposite way to her sister-in-law. She also behaves in precisely the opposite way to her mother-in-law. Naomi turns aside and pushes away; Ruth holds tight to Naomi. The Hebrew word used here of Ruth is *dabaq*, which means 'hold tight', 'be close', 'cleave', 'grasp', but it can also have an erotic or sexual meaning. For example, Genesis 2.24 says: 'Therefore a man leaves his father and mother and cleaves (*dabaq*) to his wife, and they become one flesh.' The word usually has a sexual connotation. Generally speaking, the idea of 'physical proximity' seems to underlie *dabaq*.

What does *dabaq* mean here? Does Ruth put her arm round Naomi out of compassion, or is she so strongly attached to Naomi that she never wants to leave her? And can't this attachment be described with words like 'love'? We might find an answer to these questions in Ruth's words as they are given in verses16 and 17.

1.16b   Where you go
         I will go.

Where you spend the night,
I shall spend the night.
Your people is my people,
Your God is my God.

17a   Where you die
I shall die
and there shall I be buried.

17b   Thus may YHWH do to me
and thus may he continue to do.
Nothing but death will separate me from you.

Naomi had spoken above all about herself; Ruth speaks quite explicitly about 'you and I'. Both personal pronouns occur in each clause. Moreover the whole passage sounds very like our modern marriage promise with the vow 'until death us do part'. Ruth expresses as her ardent wish that from now on she will be and remain with Naomi. She does not use the vague 'for ever', but is quite precise: she will not leave Naomi in life (16b), in death (17a), and even in the time after death, i.e. in the grave (17a). No more convincing proof of Ruth's love for Naomi is possible. The words *dabaq* and 'spend the night' could have erotic connotations. This word *dabaq* occurs three more times in the following chapters, twice with a non-sexual sense of 'attach oneself to' or 'remain close to' (2.8; 2.21) and once with the possibly sexual meaning of 'cling to' (2.22b). Therefore it is not clear to what extent there are sexual connotations in what Ruth does and states in 1.16–17. At all events, it is certain that Ruth is very attached to Naomi and loves her, for the loyalty which Ruth expresses is all-embracing and definitive. She has made her choice of Naomi: an all-determining and absolute choice which will extend from the whole of life until after death.

Ruth takes the initiative

An ardent longing combined with thoughtful words in this case shows Ruth's focus. One of her key terms is the word 'go'. Naomi constantly begs Orpah and Ruth to return to their own people in Moab, and especially to their mothers' home, so that they can again find a husband, get children and find rest. The ultimate aim is thus rest. And this rest is imagined as something to be found in familiar surroundings, with people one knows and one's own God. However, Ruth doesn't opt for this here: she wants to go away. She leaves father and mother, fatherland and mother's home behind her, and goes with Naomi, not knowing where she is going. She is taking a great risk, for while she wants to go with Naomi, she doesn't know anything about what this means. In any case, Naomi isn't very pleased, but she benefits from what is happening. The narrator says in 1.18, 'Naomi saw that Ruth was determined to *go* with her.' The difference from what Naomi said just before is obvious. There in 1.15 she had spoken of 'returning'; here the talk is of 'going'.

Ruth takes the initiative in doing something unprecedented: she gives up everything without knowing what she will get back in return. Hadn't Naomi said that she would no longer get a husband and children? 'Now I too, Ruth, will have no children. I shall not even spend the night with a man. Our fate will be the same and our lives will run in parallel. Even in our death we shall be one, and be one in our grave.' Here for Ruth the personal element of survival and a secure future, precisely what Naomi has constantly been telling her, has made a U-turn in the direction of an uncertain future. Ruth opts for Naomi, and by a word-play shows that for her there is a relationship between Naomi (*n'mi*) and 'my people' (*'mi*). Ruth's choice of Naomi at the same time implies her choice of Naomi's people.

This is Ruth's coming out, but not in the usual sense. She is coming forward, coming out as someone who is not afraid to make a leap. She takes the risk of an uncertain future in a strange land where she will live as a widow. There she will have no family of her own, and no one will know her. There she will be in a position which carries little respect with other people. She will be an outsider in every respect: as a Moabite, a woman and a widow. And she knows that Moabites are not popular in Judah. Moreover she is coming in the wake of another widow. Naomi has the advantage of being a woman of Judah, but the disadvantage of no longer having a husband, children, or the courage to live. Ruth goes, although she already knows that she will be regarded as a nameless shadow to a woman without an identity, as a woman without properties. If she is given any properties these will be the negative properties of one who is not from Judah, not a wife and not a mother.

Nevertheless, as a young widow Ruth should be able to hope for a worthy young man, a few children and a new life. However, this hope immediately goes into the ground. She excludes this possibility once and for all by saying that she will remain with Naomi not only during Naomi's lifetime but until her death. Naomi was rather older and thus could die very soon, and then Ruth would still have a whole life in front of her. Thus Ruth gives up for good the hope of belonging to another family. Since families were usually buried in one grave (hence the expression 'be buried with or gathered to one's forefathers'), Ruth is here saying that she does not want to be buried with her Moabite ancestors. Ruth's initiative is impressively absolute. Hers is a 'going' without reservations.

Ruth's faith

As well as opting for a woman and a people, at the same time Ruth opts for a God. She indicates this not only in the expression 'your God is my God' but also by actually calling on YHWH in v.17b: 'Thus may YHWH do to me and thus may he continue to do.' This verse is important if we are to understand what Ruth now really believes. Naomi believes in God on the basis of a proportionality in relations between YHWH and human beings (1.8, 13, 21); it is for YHWH to give goodness to those who show goodness. At least that is what Naomi believes. Naomi gradually distances herself from this YHWH, when first her husband and then her two children die and, old and alone, she has to go on without any future. According to Naomi, YHWH has not kept the rules fairly. And then along comes Ruth, who opts for complete surrender to YHWH. She goes with Naomi, believes in YHWH and hopes that he will be with her. She is not afraid to take the risk, though she is well aware that most people around her would prefer the certain to the uncertain and choose the familiar rather than the unknown. Precisely because she has trust in YHWH, in Naomi and in herself, she dares and promises trust. You can no longer accuse her of youthful arrogance, since she has already been married for ten years to a foreigner, a man

of Judah, and she has lost her husband. So she knows what kind
of misery life can bring. And yet this woman is ready to opt for
an uncertain future, an unknown people and an unknown God.
Ruth's trust in YHWH is not like Naomi's. Ruth does not say that
she believes in proportionality, far less does she know whether
his God will reward her for her good behaviour. He might well
not. At least he has given no sign of that in Naomi's case. And
yet Ruth believes and sets out. She cannot expect much inspira-
tion or appreciation from Naomi, yet nevertheless she does it.

Naomi is silent towards her, but will have understood her
daughter-in-law well from her own perspective and experience.
For who abandons her own family and identifies with a strange
people and a strange God? 'Your people is my people', says
Ruth to Naomi. Despite everything she believes in YHWH and
gives herself to him, without expecting to get anything out of it.
She also gives herself to Naomi without expecting anything in
return. She is not concerned primarily with investing and later
getting a good return. She invests without knowing whether
there will ever be a return at all. 'She'll have to learn and get
wiser' will have been her mother-in-law's reaction. 'Belief in
YHWH didn't do me much good and she can't expect much from
me. I'm exhausted and weary.' And yet Ruth goes, hoping for
the best!

In Ruth's own words

*I read books even before I gleaned ears of grain in Judah. And I
read and saw around me that some people make more of their
lives by having the courage to undertake something and to run
risks. They follow their longing to become better than they are.
They dare to get away from the clichés that their lives have
become. Gradually I learned that the worst choice that people
can make is not to make a choice. To continue on the familiar
cycle of life seems like the security of the warm bed that you
can't get out of the morning. The new day is cold and unknown,
and yet you have to start on it.*

*I also noted the antipathy that the otherness of aliens evokes.
I experienced it personally when I married my husband, a
foreigner from Judah. My family declared that I was crazy and*

said, 'Nothing good can come out of it; these are other people
with another culture and another God'. Sometimes it wasn't
easy, either; certainly when it seemed that I was gradually
beginning to have more of a feeling for this God of Judah. I
began to ask more and more questions about the core, the
driving force of my life. I couldn't make it out, and asked my
father and mother questions. They were annoyed with me and
called me 'Miss Clever'. Usually they didn't listen properly, but
now and then understood what I meant and got cross. I was felt
to be a threat because I asked questions about their peaceful
lives, in which there was no room for questions. They began to
avoid me, and I began to become a stranger to my own family.
And I thought that I was getting closer and closer to the people
from Judah. Perhaps that was the case as far as I was concerned, but for this family from Judah I was and remained an
outsider. They couldn't understand what I was after with all my
questions about their God and their faith. Surely I would do
better to stick to my own faith and culture? And so I was caught
between two families, in both of which everyone found it easier
to let people have their own values. At least that's what they
called it. But doesn't letting people have their own values mean
that now and then you can even share their perspectives?
And sometimes ask questions, even questions about your own
familiar situation? When confronted with that, both families
found it too threatening. They felt attacked by all these
questions. 'Leave us in peace,' they said. When first my father-
in-law and later my husband and brother-in-law died, I made
my choice: for YHWH, Judah and Naomi. My mother-in-law
didn't know what to do with me. I remained an alien to her, and
an irritating one at that. What did I want with her God, with
the God who had abandoned her, who had made her bitter and
desolate?

But I knew what I wanted. My choice was made. The very
clash between my family and that of my husband had set me
thinking years before. What did Chemosh, the God of the
Moabites, mean to me? I wasn't satisfied with the standard
answers. It was as if other people had enough answers at second
hand and didn't need their own experiences or reflections. They
got by with a vague picture of God. 'There must be something

that embraces all things,' they said, and, 'At the beginning of all creation is God. We call him Chemosh, the Mesopotamians call him Marduk, the Egyptians Ra and the people of Judah YHWH. *What difference does it make? You're a Moabite, so for you he's called Chemosh.' Therefore of course they always said 'he'. 'God dwells in you,' said others. 'So know yourself completely, and then good will come.' That's how they enjoyed life as it went fleetingly by. And they cursed God if things went badly. But most, by far the most, said, 'What a serious type you are. But don't worry. All will be well, God is on our side.' I didn't want to live that kind of life, like an armchair into which you could sink with God as a warm blanket which you could use to cover yourself.*

And I saw that the God of Judah was a different God. How different, I didn't know precisely. I assumed it, and chose on the basis of this assumption. Longing and assuming gives people a language, which doesn't say precisely what it is that's driving you, but which makes you feel what it's about. In the words which I spoke to Naomi, I tried to shape the language in order to express the things which count for me: going without expecting anything in return, trusting in the future for no reason, faithfulness without any reasonable hope of reward.

Ruth 2: The Encounter

1a   Now Naomi had a relative of her husband,
        a mighty and strong man from the same clan as Elimelek,

1b   his name was Boaz.

2a   Ruth, the Moabitess, said to Naomi,
        'I am going into the field to glean ears of grain
        after someone in whose eyes I find grace.'

2b   She said to her,
        'Go your way, my daughter.'

3a   She went
        and set out
        to glean in the field after the reapers.

3b   As chance would have it she happened on the portion of the field
        belonging to Boaz,
        who was from the same clan as Elimelek.

4a   And behold,
        Boaz came from Bethlehem
        and greeted the reapers,
        'May YHWH be with you.'

4b   They greeted him,
        'May YHWH bless you.'

5a   Boaz said to the young man who was in charge of the reapers,
        'To whom does this young woman belong?'

6a   The young man who was in charge of the reapers answered and
        said,

6b   'She is a young Moabite woman,
        who returned with Naomi from the country of Moab.

7a   She said,
        "Please let me glean
        and gather grain among the sheaves after the reapers."

7b   She came
        and she has stood waiting from early this morning until now.
        This field has been her residence.'

8a   Boaz said to Ruth,
        'Listen, my daughter,

do not go into another field to glean,
do not leave this one,

8b but stay close to my young women.

9a With your eyes on the field
where they are reaping
follow after them.
I shall order the young men
not to disturb you.

9b And if you are thirsty,
go to the vessels
and drink (the water)
that the young men have drawn.'

10a She fell on her face
and bowed to the ground.

10b She said to him,
'Why have I found grace in your eyes,
that you should take notice of me,
though I am a foreigner?'

11a Boaz replied
and said to her:
'It is told to me from all sides
all that you did for your mother-in-law after the death of
your husband,

11b that you left your father, your mother and the land of your
birth,
and have come to a people
that you did not know before.

12a May YHWH repay your action.

12b May a full reward be paid to you by YHWH the God of Israel,
under whose wings you have come to find refuge.'

13a She said,
'May I continue to find grace in your eyes, my lord,
for you have comforted me
by speaking so to the heart of your maidservant,

13b though I am not even the equal of one of your maidservants.'

14a At the mealtime Boaz said to her,
'Come here.
Eat some bread,
and dip your piece of bread in the sour wine.'

14b She went to sit with the reapers.
He offered her some roasted grain.
She ate

and was satisfied
and even had some left over.

15a   And she arose
to go and glean.

15b   Boaz commanded the young men
and said,
'She may also glean between the sheaves,
and you must not rebuke her.

16a   Moreover you must pull ears for her out of the bundles,

16b   and leave them behind
so that she can glean them,
and you must not reproach her.'

17a   And she gleaned in the field until the evening.

17b   She beat out
what she had gleaned,
and it was about an ephah of barley.

18a   She carried it
and went into the city.
Her mother-in-law saw
what she had gleaned.

18b   Thereupon she brought out and gave her
what she had left over from the meal.

19a   Her mother-in-law said to her,
'Where did you glean today,
where did you work?
Blessed be the one who took notice of you.'

19b   And she told her mother-in-law
with whom she had worked,
and she said,
'The name of the man
with whom I worked today
is Boaz.'

20a   Naomi said to her daughter-in-law,
'Blessed is he by YHWH,
for his kindness has not forsaken the living and the dead.'

20b   Naomi said to her,
'This man is a relative of ours.
He is one of those who can redeem us.'

21a   Ruth the Moabitess said,

21b   'He also said to me,
"Stay close to the young men
who are mine,

until they have finished all the harvest
which is mine." '

22a　Naomi said to Ruth her daughter-in-law,
22b　　'Good, my daughter.
　　　You must certainly go to work with his young women,
　　　　so that they do not abuse you in another field,'
23a　So she did stay close to Boaz's young women
　　　to glean until the end of the barley and the wheat harvest.
23b　And she continued to live with her mother-in-law.

Through Naomi's eyes

Naomi's knowledge

The second part of the story begins where the previous part ended. Naomi and Ruth had arrived in Bethlehem at the beginning of the barley harvest, and in this part we see the harvesting of the barley and the wheat actually taking place. The time of threshing follows in the third part, Chapter 3. Thus the agricultural seasons form the setting in which the story develops further.

As in a play, at the beginning of the second act we hear the narrator from the wings: 'Naomi had a relative or a kinsman of her husband, a mighty and strong man, and his name was Boaz.' What does the narrator really mean: does Naomi have an acquaintance or a relation? That makes a difference. The narrator uses a form derived from the verb 'know', but in Hebrew this can also mean 'know carnally' or have sexual intercourse. So he is saying that Naomi had a friend or a kinsman. At the same time the narrator is also saying something about Naomi's knowledge, namely that she knows that there is someone who is linked in one way or another to Elimelek. And this person is rich, has influence and power.

The voice goes on to say that this important man is 'from the same clan as Elimelek'. Unlike us, who only distinguish between relations and close family, at that time in Israel people distinguished a number of 'layers' within kinship relations: the innermost layer is that of the family; around it is that of the clan; and finally that of the tribe. A family was understood as the descendants of one father, and such a family was therefore called 'the house of the father', in this case the family of Elimelek. As well as that there was also a clan; this consisted of a number of families with common ancestors and was thus larger than a family. Such a clan was responsible for preserving possessions, for owning land, and the like. So Elimelek belonged to the clan of the Ephrathites. Finally came the tribe, which consisted of different clans. The clan of the Ephrathites belonged to the tribe of Judah. Boaz and Elimelek belong to the same clan and thus are not members of a family or acquaintances, but related through the clan. Naomi knows this and so now does the reader, but Ruth knows nothing of it.

Naomi's hope returns

The story only really begins in Chapter 2, after the information which the narrator gives about the figure of Boaz. It seems to have been constructed very carefully. Two conversations between Ruth and Naomi form the opening and closing scenes, and in between come the events in the field. At the heart of it stand the dialogues between Boaz and Ruth. Everything seems to turn on the encounter between these two, at which Naomi is not present. Does that mean that from now on Naomi fades into the background or is even displaced, whereas in the previous chapter she was the pivot around which everything turned? No, that is certainly not the case. The conversation between Naomi and Ruth at the end of the narrative is too important for that.

The opening conversation between Ruth and Naomi is of no great importance. Naomi reacts to Ruth's proposal to go gleaning and says, 'Go your way, my daughter' (2.2). Ruth does not ask her consent, but does get approval from Naomi, who is also no longer as grumpy as before. She seems to think that what's done is done and that's that. She herself doesn't undertake anything, but she doesn't prevent Ruth from doing something. In the end of the day, someone must get them something to eat. The only thing that she says is 'Go'. Perhaps she could have warned Ruth that as a solitary woman and above all as a foreigner she was in danger, and could become the victim of offensive remarks or even molestation. But she does not do so, and Ruth goes her way.

Only at the end of the day does Naomi see what has happened to Ruth during the day. She sees the great quantity of grain that Ruth brings home with her. An ephah of grains of barley; that's a whole basketful! How did she get it? You can almost see Naomi's eyes popping open with amazement. It's the first good thing that has happened to her for ages. After that she speaks four times (in verses 19, 20a, 20b and 22), and each time there is more of a glow in her eyes. The journey up from the deep valley of despair seems to have begun.

Her surprise becomes even greater when Ruth conjures up not only the basketful of grain but also a handful of remnants from the midday meal. After all the grain, Naomi is already thinking, 'How can anyone glean so much by herself in one day?'. From the remnants of the prepared meal she grasps that Ruth cannot have done this all by herself. Someone must have helped her. Moreover she asks, 'What have you gathered today, where did you work?' Naomi is so excited that she even asks the same question twice: where, tell me where in the world have you been today? Even before Ruth has an opportunity to reply, the excited Naomi has already spoken a blessing over Ruth's bene-factor. She doesn't even know the name of the person, but she wishes him the best: 'Blessed be the one who took notice of you.' All the emphasis is on the unknown Mr X who 'saw you', 'noticed you', or 'paid attention to you'. Although Naomi doesn't know it, here she is using the same word that Ruth had used earlier in her conversation with Boaz ('Why should you take notice of me?') (2.10). What she does know is that the one who noticed an alien is worthy of respect, a man of worth. It doesn't matter that she doesn't yet know his name, since what she blesses him for is his 'taking notice'.

Ruth then gets an opportunity to relate what has happened to her, and right at the end of the story she mentions the name of the man concerned: his name is Boaz. The name means nothing to Ruth, but it does to Naomi. It immediately provokes a reaction from her, and for the second time she blesses him, now that she knows his name: 'Blessed is Boaz by YHWH.'

Kinship and law through Naomi's eyes

For the third time Naomi reacts to Ruth's report that Boaz is the man who helped her. Ruth doesn't get a word in edgeways, and Naomi goes on without taking breath. The important remark comes out: 'This man is near or a kinsman to us. He is one of those who can redeem us' (2.20b). Ruth did not grasp why Naomi was so excited when she heard the name of Boaz. Now she understands: this man is a member of the clan. But why isn't Naomi more precise: he is 'near', but we don't yet know the precise relationship between her and Boaz. The narrator was also just as unclear when he was speaking of Boaz as 'someone from the clan of Elimelek'. So what is he? An uncle, a great-uncle, a grandnephew, a great-grandnephew, or a great-grand-nephew of a great uncle? However, Naomi is clear about something else when she says that he is a relative of 'ours' and that he is one of 'our' redeemers. For the first time she shows that she definitively regards Ruth as a member of the family.

But what is a redeemer? The term *go'el* which is used in the Hebrew comes from Israelite family law: a *go'el* or redeemer is a relative who has particular obligations within a clan. If someone has to sell his land out of economic need, a *go'el* is the one in the clan who is responsible for buying back the land so that the clan heritage remains intact. Or if someone is so poor that he has to sell himself as a slave, a *go'el* is the one who redeems that member of the clan. A *go'el* is the member of the clan who avenges the murder of a relative by killing the murderer or sees to reparations when injustice is done. So there are even more cases in which within the clan the *go'el* is the person who on the basis of solidarity mends the breaches in the life or the possessions of his kinsfolk. If such a break is repaired, then the clan's bond or wholeness is repaired. So you could call a redeemer a 'clan-mender' or 'bandager'. Of course there is not just one redeemer in a clan: anyone who has a particular degree of kinship to another and is financially in a position to do so, can come forward as a redeemer to help a member of the clan who has been victimized. The closer the relationship, the stronger is the obligation to redeem. So there are many possible redeemers, but the only actual redeemer is the one who repairs the break that has come about.

Thus far Ruth does not realize that Boaz is a relative, far less that he is a redeemer. When Naomi hears the name Boaz, she immediately connects it with her knowledge that Boaz is a kinsman of Elimelek. She thinks that she can refer to the right of redemption that applies within the clan. At the same time it becomes clear to the readers why the relationship has been spoken of in such vague terms. This does not give us any picture of the precise relationship between Naomi and Boaz. Had we known what it was, we could have inferred from it the degree of obligation which Boaz had to Naomi. That this obligation is not very great and that Naomi does not immediately have the right to redemption emerges not only from the terms 'acquaintance from the clan of' and 'near', but also from the fact that Naomi has not appealed to Boaz earlier. Nor has Boaz himself offered help, despite the fact that he knows of Elimelek's death and the return of his widow (2.11). So Boaz is not immediately obliged to help, for had he been, he would have been in breach of his obligation to help. That is the precise point on which this question turns: it is Naomi who concentrates on the right of redemption within the clan, although Boaz has no obligations to her because of his vague clan relationship. Through Ruth's answer Naomi sees in a flash the possibility of making an appeal to this right, since although Boaz has no obligations, he is certainly in a position to redeem. He does not need to, but he can.

In the first chapter Naomi had lost everything and blamed YHWH for this. She had the feeling that YHWH had withheld his justice from her and had failed her. Now all at once she sees hope dawning. She senses that within the rules of the clan she can appeal to Boaz's obligation to act as redeemer. Naomi tends to see things as law which, as emerges clearly here, are not based purely on law but also on good will or are voluntary. Perhaps that is the difference between Naomi and Ruth: Ruth does not have the feeling that she is right. Sometimes when Ruth has had a positive encounter, she has the feeling of having been given it freely. By contrast Naomi, is someone who believes in fairness and a just order. When she is being treated badly by the standards of this order, she feels injured and thinks that the hand of YHWH has acted unreasonably heavily towards her. When she was treated well by this standard, namely when Ruth even went with her, she was very surprised and even somewhat off-putting. Ruth had no obligation whatsoever to go with her; indeed it was to her own disadvantage. Her behaviour was out of proportion. And Naomi likes right proportions, order and justice.

For Naomi, everything is also different from what it is for Ruth. Naomi stands within a group which protects her; she has rights. Ruth is a foreigner and stands outside the family law of Israel. Nor is she assured of support. As a foreigner she stands outside any order, for order aims at protecting one's own group. It is the narrator who makes this clear to us in the next line (2.21a). Naomi has not yet said 'he is near to us and one of our redeemers' when the narrator says, 'Ruth, the *Moabitess*, said.' Ruth was last called 'Moabitess' at the beginning of Chapter 2. After that she increasingly became 'Naomi's daughter-in-law'. But at the precise moment when Naomi puts all the emphasis on family ties and recognizes Ruth completely as a member of the family, the narrator puts Ruth in her place. There is no rebuke to Ruth, at most to Naomi, in the sense of, 'Just don't count on it too much; she is and remains a foreigner.' Moreover Ruth's next remark and Naomi's reaction to it are about the danger that such a foreign woman risks in the fields.

This is the last time that Naomi speaks in this chapter. She says: 'Good, my daughter. You must certainly go to work with his young women, so that they do not abuse you in another field' (2.22). The first time that Ruth announced that she was going gleaning (2.2) Naomi simply said, 'Go your way, my daughter.' Then she agreed with Ruth but did not warn her. Now that she is more involved, she has hope and perspective again (and for this she needs Ruth). She warns Ruth about the risks that a foreign woman runs in a strange field. Men can pester any woman, but a foreigner has no one behind her. That the problems can be great emerges from the words 'attack' or 'assault' that Naomi uses here. Ruth the Moabite woman runs a real risk in such a field, and assault is a real threat. We had just forgotten the ethnic differences and had above all felt the togetherness between Naomi and Ruth. The narrator and Naomi themselves draw our attention to the fact that Ruth, the foreign woman, has no protection and cannot be certain of anything.

In Naomi's own words

I have to confess something. I thought that this woman, my daughter-in-law, was just like these other foreigners. But I was wrong. She's a good exception. She's a Moabite woman, but in her heart she's a woman of Judah. Just look at her faith: she believes in YHWH *and looks after me well. Many scribes have also described it like this: Ruth was already a woman of Judah in her heart while she was still in Moab, and so she could also begin to belong to the Jewish people. By this they meant that Ruth was not really accepted into our people as a Moabite woman, but as one who believed in* YHWH. *So one doesn't have to put too much emphasis on her alien features, but on those in which she's like us. Ruth is a special woman, unique for a Moabite. So don't think that I believe that all these Moabites should be able to come here; I don't think that at all.*

First I thought that Ruth was different from us, a bit strange and so on. I thought that she was too stupid to be true, but I underestimated her. She's not so different; now she's even part of our family. Normally I don't believe in that sort of thing, that someone can marry into a family; usually those who marry in are mere appendages. Although I certainly feel part of the clan of Elimelek; but that's different. They, I mean the Moabites, are unbelievers, and we aren't. There's nothing for them here. Despite the fact that she was an alien, Ruth was accepted into our people because she believed in the true God. That's how it is with us: anyone who believes in YHWH *and behaves accordingly, belongs.*

'Would I also be so open to other foreigners?', you ask. That depends. If they want to live here in Judah they have to adapt to us and not keep their strange customs and beliefs. They can hardly ask our religion to allow other people to believe in another God. Don't you believe that your God is the one true God? If you want to accept foreigners, they have to understand

that our rules are also the rules which they need to keep, that our God is their God. If they do that they can certainly stay. For we're tolerant; we're known for that. Anyone who is ready to adapt and recognize that our order is the right one, that our law is God's law, may begin to be part of us. And if they're part of us, they aren't alien or other any more; they've become like us. That's integration, isn't it? Everyone keeps talking about that. Oh, is integration that these other people may also stay different? I didn't know that, and I don't think much of it. I'm not talking about Ruth, you know; she's a good sound girl. All along she's been a good believer in her heart and truly one of us.

But that doesn't mean that we must immediately let all those Moabites in, with that dirty eating and those funny clothes. Do you know how these people pray? They sit down when they pray. Everyone knows that you pray standing up. I've even heard that there are people who do it kneeling. Wonders will never cease. And then should we allow all those Moabites in, with that strange language of theirs? We would even become aliens in our own land. It's easy for you to talk, you live in the area where the villas are. You don't see these people all day. But we ordinary people have them all around us. Perhaps they should open a reception centre for Moabites in the empty villa next to you. Oh, you've already bought it up. You say you need the room. For the children, then they will have more room to play. Yes, I get it. And you talk about real integration, preserving one's own identity, while you live in a detached house? Who knows these foreigners better, you or I? Indeed, I've lived in Moab myself, for more than ten years. How was I treated there? Well, we had no complaints. We didn't trouble ourselves with them and usually went our own way. Yes, certainly that sounds inconsistent, when I want them to adapt to us and we didn't do that in Moab. But that's not the case. Here it's very different. Bethlehem is a small town and you must take account of one another. I object to these foreigners if they don't adapt to us here and if they continue to worship these strange gods. That's not on. Take it from me, it's best for them to act like Ruth and to begin to believe in YHWH. *Otherwise they should stay where they come from.*

Through Boaz's eyes

The introduction of Boaz

A new figure is introduced to the readers in 2.1. It is Boaz, a member of the same clan as Elimelek. Naomi already knows him, and the reader has got to know him through her eyes. He has been called an *ish gibbor chayil*. An *ish* is a man; a *gibbor* is a brave hero in war, a strong man in the city gate, or a rich man, respected and influential. A *chayil* is someone with great physical strength or a powerful personality. So an *ish chayil* can be both an Arnold Schwarzenegger and a strong personality. Probably this is not a description of Boaz's muscles, but more of his power and the strength of his personality: Boaz is powerful and strong, rich and influential, respected and with an impressive personality. His name emphasizes this, because 'Boaz' means 'in him is strength'. As readers of verse 1 we do not yet know what kind of a profession this powerful man has, whether he's married, or whether he himself knows of his clan relationship with Naomi.

We soon learn more about his profession. He has a farm, as is clear from v.3b: 'And as chance would have it, Ruth was on the portion of the field belonging to Boaz, who was of the same clan as Elimelek.' Boaz is the owner of the land on which Ruth wants to glean. Ruth doesn't yet know whose the land is or who Boaz is, far less does Boaz know who she is. The way in which they both meet on the field is completely by chance. Many people, including exegetes, tend to call this providence. The text itself speaks only of 'chance'. The unity of time and place makes the lines of the two main characters cross.

There are other figures on the field, the reapers. They are greeted by the owner, Boaz, with 'May YHWH be with you.' This greeting is in a way comparable to 'The Lord be with you' in church. They reply, 'May YHWH bless you', an equivalent of 'And with your spirit'. They all prove to be believers in YHWH. The blessing said by the reapers recalls that of Naomi later, in 2.20: 'He is blessed before YHWH.' Evidently it is usual to wish someone YHWH's blessing. These greetings and wishes are not empty formulae, but expressions of faith which function in daily life. As well as being a relative of Elimelek and a

landowner, here Boaz is now also introduced as a believer in
YHWH. Moreover we, too, should look at Boaz from these three
perspectives.

Boaz the boss

In the conversation with his overseer and his servants in the field
Boaz is clearly the boss: he gives orders, asks questions, regu-
lates and organizes. He looks over the field the moment he
arrives and makes the foreman responsible for what is going on.
He does so with a short question, 'To whom does the young
woman belong?' (2.5). And the overseer embarks on a long
story. It's as if he has to make excuses. Boaz's question is
characteristic of this time: a woman is not independent but
belongs to someone else, or even is someone else's. At that
moment, for Boaz, Ruth is like all other women. That changes
after the foreman's answer. The first thing that he says is, 'This
woman is a Moabitess', since the fact that she comes from
abroad is of course the most striking thing about her. But as an
alien, she is not completely alone in the world, since she belongs
to Naomi. Moreover the overseer says that she has returned
with Naomi from the land of Moab. Again he mentions the
name Moab: a Moabitess from Moab – where else would she
come from? He is evidently fascinated by a woman from Moab
who comes to Judah. He even uses the word 'return' for Ruth.
In Chapter 1 the narrator had shown that Naomi was returning,
whereas Ruth was going away and not returning. But of course
this overseer doesn't know that.

The foreman goes further and even describes at length what
Ruth had said and done: she asked whether she might glean,
whether she might collect the ears behind the reapers, and since
then she has been standing there waiting. The foreman has not
dared to answer her question and asks himself again, and
perhaps also anxiously, how Boaz will react. Boaz is a friendly
man, but he is the boss. He doesn't tell the foreman what to do
with Ruth, but himself turns to Ruth who is waiting patiently. A
conversation develops between Boaz and Ruth which Boaz
starts and in which he has by far the most to say. He speaks to
Ruth in a friendly way, but distances himself a bit. The first

thing he advises her is, 'Don't go away from this field'. To advise someone about what he or she was already planning is a well-tried means of establishing your authority. Then he says what Ruth must do, namely remain with the women in this field, keep her eyes on the field and gather ears of grain. Keeping one's eyes on the field is a somewhat superfluous addition. How else is one to glean? Boaz is thus a well-meaning boss, a bit fussy, as a boss should be. He gives her permission in the form of an order.

Then he goes a step further. Boaz puts her under his protection and tells the men to give the order that she is not to be molested. That is surprising, since hitherto she has not seemed to be threatened by any danger. Evidently it was not so safe to let a solitary (foreign) women do such lowly work. Moreover he shows that he realizes that Ruth cannot work in the heat without anything to drink. Normally you would have to get yourself a drink from a well. He allows her to drink from the jars. In this respect she is treated as one of his employees. But not otherwise, since of course she remains a gleaner who perhaps may come close to the others but must keep behind them. So Boaz gives an extended and positive answer to Ruth's question expressed indirectly through the foreman. His style and verbosity perhaps indicate his age, or otherwise his great power or perhaps his good mood, or . . . His motives are unknown. All that we know is that in any case he is not hard up and is well disposed to her.

Ruth shows her relief: 'Why have I found grace in your eyes?', and Boaz then tells her that he has already heard about her and her good deeds. When the overseer spoke about a Moabite woman who had come with Naomi he could evidently associate information that he had been given previously with her. Boaz then expresses the wish that YHWH will recompense her work and fully reward her (2.12). Twice here in Hebrew we have the root *shalem*, pay out or pay back, a term from economics which later also took on the transferred meaning of 'complete, fulfil', as in *shalom*: fullness or peace. Boaz the landowner and businessman speaks here of YHWH's reward in terms of wages and payment. Just as Boaz pays their wages to his workers, so he hopes that God will pay Ruth. Clearly, with his assent Boaz wants to reward Ruth for what she did for

Naomi. But at the same time he is aware that he cannot settle the whole account. Hence his wish for YHWH to repay her fully for all her good deeds.

After that, presumably everyone sets to work. The narrator does not say anything about this, but he leaves a gap; he is above all interested in the dialogues. Towards the meal time we return to the field, when Boaz calls Ruth and allows her to go and sit with the workers. To give an impression of a possible division of time: if Ruth had arrived around five in the morning and Boaz appeared around eight, then she had to stand waiting for three hours. After Boaz's consent she went to work until the midday meal, probably around twelve or one; thus she had already been standing bent over in the field in the burning sun for four hours. The narrator does not have much of an eye for practical details, and does not tells us anything unless it serves a particular function. So he does relate that Boaz allows Ruth to share the bread and also to dip the bread in the sour, refreshing wine. That is a privilege, since it emerges from this that Boaz is treating Ruth as one of his employees. He even goes a step further and offers her roasted grain, i.e. grain roasted on an iron plate (the popcorn of that time). That is something special, for the boss to offer something to someone who is lower than his servants. After the meal, Boaz goes so far as to order the reapers not to prevent Ruth if she looks for ears between the sheaves. They must even take ears from the sheaves and leave them behind for her. That is exceptional. Normally gleaners were not allowed to go into the part where the reaping had been done but the sheaves had not been bound. No one was allowed to go between the bundles or sheaves of cut grain. Nor did the reapers normally leave ears behind on purpose. Boaz allows Ruth this in a generous gesture, a gesture which surpasses all that has gone before. It is an unprecedented initiative on the part of Boaz, and the servants are amazed, as are the readers. Is Boaz going to be more than a businessman and a boss? Does he have other plans for Ruth?

Boaz charmed by Ruth

Boaz is more than just a boss who is responsible for his land and harvest. To see that, for the fun of it one need only underline how often the terms 'young men' (*na'arim*) and 'young women' (*na'arot*) appear in this chapter. One then discovers that Boaz differs from the others not only by virtue of his power and the land that he owns, but also by virtue of his age. That begins immediately after Boaz appears on the stage in verse 4 and addresses 'the young man who was appointed over the reapers'. Not once but twice we have this periphrasis for what can be described in the one word 'foreman' or 'overseer'. This man is not only Boaz's senior servant in the fields, but also a young man. When Boaz asks the young foreman (*na'ar*) 'to whom the young woman (*na'ara*) belongs', his question implies that the young woman, Ruth, is about the same age as the young man. The young man's answer indicates this: 'She (= Ruth) is a young Moabite woman.' The word *na'ara*, which is used twice for Ruth, means 'servant' or 'unmarried (and thus marriageable) young woman'. So the factor of being of a marriageable age certainly plays a role here: Ruth is a marriageable young woman, and the foreman is a marriageable young man. And what about Boaz? He is a strong and powerful man, but of a different age. The workers in the field, the foreman and Ruth are all young people of the same age, whereas Boaz is much older.

That difference in age also emerges in Boaz's words. Like Naomi, he calls her 'my daughter'. In Naomi's mouth this seems to derive from the family link between the two. Now that Boaz also uses this form of address a number of times, we get the impression that it has more to do with age. Because Boaz and Naomi belong to the same age-group, they can address the much younger Ruth as 'my daughter', and at the same time expresses not only concern but also a form of distancing in age. 'Listen, my daughter, do not ever go from here, but stay close to my young women' (2.8). Boaz is urging Ruth to stay with his young women. For this he uses the word *dabaq*, the same word that the narrator had used in 1.14 to describe Ruth's staying firmly with Naomi. However, in 1.14 *dabaq* was used in combination with the preposition *be*, which means 'cling to', whereas here in 2.8 *dabaq* is used in combination with the preposition *im*, which means 'keep close by'. At the same time Boaz promises Ruth that he will give the young men orders not to disturb her, as indeed he does later. It is all the more remarkable that on her return from the field, Ruth tells Naomi that Boaz had urged her to 'stick close to the young men' (2.21). But Boaz had never said that. He said, 'Remain close to the young women, then I shall see to it that the young men stay away.' In reacting to Ruth, Naomi says the same thing as Boaz: 'Go with his young women, so that they (masculine plural) do not abuse you in another field' (2.22b). Boaz had talked about the young men 'disturbing' and 'annoying' her. Naomi speaks of 'abusing' or 'assaulting'. In the eyes of the older people the threat posed by the young men is very great.

Does Boaz consciously or unconsciously have other intentions for Ruth? Generally speaking, erotic feelings are not disturbing at any age. Or is Boaz solely concerned, as older paternal men often are, to offer protection to the young women, because they know the wicked outside world and the young women do not? Probably the two do not rule each other out. Boaz's increasingly good disposition towards Ruth and above all his unprecedented command to take ears from the sheaves and leave them for her could indicate that he is not only concerned for her but also attracted to her to some degree. There is something else that suggests ambiguity in Boaz's action, namely what he says in v.11b. There he remarks, 'You have left your father and mother.' This is presumably a quotation from the well-known text of Genesis 2.24: 'Therefore a man leaves his father and his mother and cleaves (*dabaq be*) to his wife and they become one flesh.' Shortly beforehand, Boaz had been telling Ruth that she must remain close to (*dabaq 'im*) his young women and Ruth summed that up by saying that 'she had to remain close to (*dabaq be*) the young men'. So the reader gets the impression that either the narrator or Ruth and Boaz are providing an undercurrent here, which confirms the thought that Boaz is occupied in more than just organizing his agricultural affairs. Boaz need not be aware of all this. Ruth seems to be more aware of it, as is indicated by the cunning rephrasing in her conversation with Naomi. In her quotation of what Boaz says she changes the young women into young men and *dabaq im*, keep close to, into *dabaq be*, attach oneself to. Naomi's reaction ('My daughter, go with his young women') gives the impression that they each have their own suspicions. Sometimes young women know more about the wicked world outside than their fathers think. Sometimes old women only need one line to weave a net.

Boaz's view of life and his faith

Other aspects of Boaz's views of life and God, a life which does not of course consist only of work and love, become evident in what he says, especially to Ruth. Thus in v.11 he evaluates what Ruth has done, and in v.12 he indicates what God has to do with it. Both aspects call for separate attention.

Boaz sums up Ruth's behaviour like this:

2.11a   It is told to me from all sides
         all that you did for your mother-in-law after the death of your
            husband,
11b   that you left your father, your mother and the land of your
            birth,
         and have come to a people
         that you did not know before.

Boaz is aware of what Ruth has done, that she has abandoned everything for the sake of her mother-in-law. No one had seen or said that so far: neither Naomi, the narrator, nor even Ruth herself. It is fascinating to see how the word for 'leave behind' or 'abandon', the Hebrew word *'azab*, keeps appearing in Chapters 1 and 2. In 1.16 Ruth says that Naomi must not force her to follow her sister-in-law and leave Naomi behind or abandon her. In 2.11b Boaz recognizes that Ruth has left behind her father and her mother and the land of her birth in order to go to Naomi's people. Here Boaz precisely brings out the crucial point in Ruth's behaviour: her going necessarily involves leaving others behind. By going away she leaves the familiar behind her, and by going with Naomi she does not leave something or someone else behind. In Hebrew, *'azab* and *dabaq (be)*, leave and cling to, are two sides of the same coin, namely the coin of choice. Thus choosing is not just fine, pleasant, attractive, but is indissolubly bound up with the pain caused by leaving behind something familiar. Boaz's reference to Genesis 2.24 is of fundamental importance in this respect, since precisely there it becomes evident that the man who cleaves to his wife (*dabaq*) leaves his father and mother (*'azab*). Genesis and Boaz recognize that the two aspects are connected.

The word *'azab* occurs twice more. In 2.16 Boaz says to the reapers that they must leave behind ears and in 2.20 Naomi gives her final verdict on Boaz: 'for his kindness has not forsaken the living and the dead' (2.20). According to Naomi, Boaz, *b'z*, does not do any *'zb* (with vowels, *'azab*). Thus the play on the word *'azab* is extended. Ruth leaves her father and mother behind, but does not abandon Naomi. Boaz leaves ears of corn behind, but does not abandon the living and the dead. This leaving behind and abandoning is regularly expressed by one word, *'azab*. And it is Boaz who has an eye for the twofold aspect of this *'azab*. He sees that going always involves a leaving behind, whereas returning does not. He himself has not run such a risk a Ruth, since leaving behind a few ears of corn is not comparable to leaving one's father and mother. Probably a difference can be indicated here between Boaz and Naomi. Naomi clings more to the familiar and argues more for returning than for going (away). Boaz himself does not give up the familiar, but sees Ruth's choice and going (with) in a positive light.

In v.12 Boaz connects all this with his faith in God:

2.12a   May YHWH repay your action.
12b   May a full reward be paid to you by YHWH the God of Israel, under whose wings you have come to find refuge.

Boaz says that YHWH will reward Ruth for her choice of Naomi. This is a wish and not a certainty, expressed in terms of recompense. Boaz's image of God is like that of Naomi: his God is a God of order, of fairness and equilibrium, *shalom*. So he uses the term *shalem* twice: Ruth has done good, has taken a risk and opted for YHWH; he will repay (*shalem*) her efforts and recompense (*shalem*) her. In Chapter 1 Naomi's wish for her daughters-in-law had been that 'YHWH will do good to you, as you have done good to the dead and to me' (1.8). The way this is put by Boaz, who was not present at the events in Chapter 1 and thus did not hear what Naomi said either, resembles Naomi's expression. Both express the wish that someone who does good shall be rewarded by YHWH's goodness. However, in the Hebrew Boaz also offers a variation: Naomi praised Ruth and Orpah because they had done good to the dead and to her. Boaz praises 'all that you have done for your mother-in-law (*ch.mot.h*) since the death (*mot*) of your husband'. He is no longer talking about the dead (*mot*), but about the mother-in-law (*ch.mot.h*), and by opting for her mother-in-law Ruth is opting for both the dead and for the living and not just for the living.

Ruth opts for YHWH, whom Boaz describes as 'the God of Israel'. She has not sought refuge with Chemosh, the God of the Moabites, as might have been expected; nor with Molech, the God of the Ammonites; nor with Ashtoreth, the God of the Sidonians; nor with Baal-Zebub, the God of the Ekronites, but with YHWH, the God of the Israelites. So YHWH will offer her protection. We find the same expression, 'seek refuge under (the shadow of) the wings of YHWH', in the Psalms (91.4; 57.2; 61.5). In this sense v.12b is a conventional religious expression, not invented by Boaz but applied by him to Ruth. In other words, Boaz is reacting to Ruth's bold enterprise with religious texts, one of which goes back to Genesis 2.24 and one to the Psalms. He sees what Ruth has done, recognizes that *'azab* and *dabaq*, leaving and clinging to, go together, and expresses the wish that YHWH will again bring order and offer protection. Boaz is certainly no revolutionary, so his wishes smack too much of a restoration of the old and familiar order. He is a good, conservative man.

The God of (one's own) order has many faces. Naomi longs for rest and security. But she is also on the bad side of society. She has suffered emotional blows by losing her husband and her children and has also suffered financially, so that it is difficult for her to keep her head above water. She no longer sees a future, has no expectation or hope. Like Naomi, Boaz likes a good balance, *shalom*. Who doesn't?, one might think. What is more desirable than for good deeds to be repaid by God, and for there to be a connection between action and reward? But unlike Naomi, Boaz is on the good, rich side of society. He has not suffered any personal loss, and is better able to withstand a financial loss. He can even be bothered about aliens or foreigners as long as they do not disturb his order, but adapt to it. He is perhaps the civilized inhabitant of a villa area with a social conscience whom I conjured up in Naomi's words. He appreciates stability, trusts in a God who protects good order and is sympathetic to those who are bowed down under a heavy burden. He is not himself assailed by misery. Nevertheless, he is aware of his responsibility for law and justice. He can see Ruth's risky departure in a positive light because he himself does not need to give up everything and go. His familiar surroudings are good. Ruth, still a couple of steps lower in the social order, may be accepted into these familiar surroundings. She may seek protection under the wings of his God. The wings of this God are wide enough for all.

Modern readers do not find it difficult to feel some affinity to Boaz. Not because his option is the best, but because it matches our situation in the rich West now: being open to foreigners who have fled, without needing to give up our familiar surroundings and prosperity. Ruth is admirable for doing this, for taking a risk on the basis of a deliberate choice: for someone, her mother-in-law; for a land, Judah; and for a God, YHWH, without being certain that order, equilibrium, will result. Those who know how the story goes on can simply say that it turns out well. But who dares to say that to the boat people from Haiti who flee to Florida, or to the Somalis who flee to the Netherlands, or to the Bosnians who flee to Germany? Perhaps death by drowning, refugee camps or social chaos awaits them. They may never recover. Their flight to our country does not attack our order; they will have to adapt to our society and norms. It is not difficult to accept someone like Ruth, since she has recognized and adopted Boaz's own order, the order of Judah. Therefore it is also easy to adopt her. Moreover Boaz can express his hope for a restoration of good order, but it is his order. He is making his own contribution, but his faith and view of life are not essentially being attacked; his order is not being threatened by aliens. Possibly things will be difficult for him, too, in the future.

In Boaz's own words

What more do I want? I'm rich and own a great estate. My servants are devoted to me, and my land produces a good harvest. I know that this isn't all thanks to me and my efforts, and moreover I thank God every day for all the good things that he has given me. I'm also aware that my weak point is that I work much too hard, so that I don't do many other things. They call me a workaholic, but I usually enjoy my work, although sometimes it gets rather out of hand. Especially at harvest time I just keep working. Now and then I'm overcome by sleep even on the threshing floor. On the other hand, as a result of my work and money I'm in a position to do something for other people. Poor people can come and work for me. If they take on the reaping, they're assured of a daily meal and an honest wage. Strangers always find lodging with me and then they often ask me whether I'm married. My answer is always, 'I'm married to my work, my land and my people.' Now and then I hear rumours going around that 'he may well be homosexual'. People have to do something to fill their day. They ask what my secret is: 'Perhaps he was once unlucky in love, or who knows, he may have a love elsewhere, possibly . . .' They keep on fantasizing, but it doesn't hurt me. I feel more at home in the senate, in the assembly of the elders. There I'm in my place. Over the years I've become more experienced and have learned the rules of the game. I'm well aware that despite all the rules, only honesty and justice count. Certainly I enjoy speaking in public and like to hold people when I'm on the public tribune, but it's also important to apply the law honestly and promote a wise government.

At night when it's quiet and I'm lying in bed alone, I feel rather lonely. It's not just the need for a woman (yes, I'm heterosexual) or a warm body, but above all the longing for children, for a family, to have some one standing beside me. In short, I don't want to be alone everywhere. But when day comes I usually shake off the darkness of the night and set to work energetically. To achieve and do something gives much satisfaction. It's great to see something growing under your hands; it's good to be of help to others. But the crazy thing is that as I get older, restless dreams constantly disturb my night's rest. Almost every week I have a dream that a tree is growing around me with fruit on it. Oh, I don't need to be a Freudian to know what this means. But these dreams disturb me and often after such a night I get up more tired than when I went to bed. They exhaust me, but I don't plan to burden others with them.

Yesterday something strange happened to me. The early morning was as it always is. I had shaved, cleaned my teeth and combed my grey hair, and after a light breakfast had gone to my fields where the barley harvest was being gathered in. My overseer had told me the day before, 'It's a good harvest this year, and fortunately we've enough workers.' I agreed with him. My eye fell on a face that I hadn't seen before. 'Who's that there?', I asked him, pointing to a woman who was standing watching a little way off. She stood very still, a picture of rest. She was still a young woman, and the early morning cold didn't seem to affect her. 'I don't know her name,' said the overseer. 'She speaks with a foreign accent. She's a Moabitess, who has come back with Naomi her mother-in-law.' 'I'll go over to her. You get on with your work,' I said, and I thought, 'What an attractive girl!' At that moment I heard a cry. One of the reapers had hurt himself and I ran up the field. A bit later a wagon wheel broke and someone had to be got quickly from the village to repair it. And that's how the morning went.

Around the time of the midday meal, I noticed the foreign woman again. Not that she said much; on the contrary, she was silence personified. The young men tried to bring her out a bit, but she paid no attention. The other girls giggled and reacted more knowingly to the challenges of the young men. It irritated me somewhat, all that noise. 'Leave that child alone,' I told them. But you know what these young people are. Yes, I'm becoming a real old bore. I'm not her anxious father and she's already been a married woman for many years. Fortunately I restrained myself and muttered to myself, 'Man, what are you doing?' When immediately afterwards I gave her some roasted grain, a delicacy for which our district is famous, I saw the others looking amazed. It was certainly rather unusual for me to do that. A little later I ordered my servants, when they got back to reaping, deliberately to let some barley drop for this woman.

They couldn't believe their ears; I saw them thinking, 'Now the boss has gone crazy.' Perhaps they're right. Something in me is touched by this woman, though I don't know what. Heavens above, surely I'm not falling in love with such a young woman in my old age?

Through Ruth's eyes

A foreigner between courage and humiliity

From Ruth's perspective, everything looks quite different. After departing from the land of her birth, she has arrived in an alien environment. She does not know anyone but her mother-in-law. But hardly has she arrived in Bethlehem than she immediately goes into the fields. It's harvest time. Why didn't Naomi go with her? 'Going' is not for Naomi, who hitherto has wanted only to return: it's always Ruth who goes. How remarkable her initiative and her courage is gradually becomes clear. From the beginning the narrator calls her 'the Moabitess'. Her ethnic origin marks her out in Bethlehem. But she sets aside any anxiety about being discriminated against as a Moabitess and takes the risk. She goes to the fields where grain is being gathered and the harvest is now in full swing. She runs a risk there not only as a Moabitess but also as a woman, since despite the right to glean behind the binders, women were often molested, assaulted or abducted when in the fields. And a right anchored in the law does not of itself assure security or safety. As well as being threatened by racial tensions or the dangers to which women are exposed, Ruth is under threat as a 'loose woman' in a patriarchal society in which only women who are tied to a man are fully respected. Ruth is in the weakest position conceivable, and yet has the courage to do something.

Once she has arrived at a field she sees how the work is done. The men are reaping: they keep cutting handfuls of grain and putting them down in rows. After them come the women who gather these rows into sheaves or bundles, and after that the sheaves are brought to the threshing floor. Good reapers and binders leave little behind, yet after them come various poor women, above all widows. They gather all the loose ears and grains which the others have left behind. Gleaning is a matter of peering and looking, standing bent over and searching, yet it doesn't produce much. A whole day's hard toil for a handful of grains of corn is work that requires a great deal of humility. Ruth wants to ask permission for this work and would be happy if she gets it. She even calls it a grace for which she hopes. At first sight that seems almost too humble: officially she doesn't even need to ask for consent, since to glean ears of grain is the right of the poor and widows. Probably as a foreign widow she wants to be completely sure. How will the Bethlehemites look on such a woman, such a strange person? Will they see only her headscarf? At all events, it is clear from v.2a that she is well aware of her weak position. But she shows remarkable courage. Perhaps if you're weaker you also have to be much more courageous than if you're a strong person.

Ruth asks permission from the overseer, but we readers only hear that later:

2.7a   (the overseer said,)
        'She said,
            "Please let me glean
            and gather grain among the sheaves after the reapers."
7b   She came
        and she has stood waiting from early this morning until now.
        This field has been her residence.'

Thus it is usual for poor women to go behind the reapers and behind the women making sheaves in order to glean grain. However, Ruth asks whether she may look for ears among the sheaves. That is an unprecedented question, but it is quite understandable: if she goes along the rows which the women are still putting into sheaves, at all events she will be one of the first gleaners and she will be able to find more. This woman is brave! In place of the stereotyped picture of Ruth, here we see a bold woman. The overseer cannot give her permission and waits for the boss to come. Meanwhile Ruth waits patiently, hour after hour. 'It's as though she lives here,' says the overseer mockingly. And then the boss, Boaz, comes and says yes: she may go between the rows and sheaves. He makes it clear indirectly that this is a favour, which he makes even greater by ordering the reapers to drop ears for her. Ruth's boldness is rewarded. Ruth doesn't seem to be a timid girl, but she is well aware of what is not permissible to ask for. Patience and resolution characterize her to a considerable degree.

From going to waiting

This Ruth is an enterprising woman. She is beginning something new and gets on with it steadily. The others, Boaz, the foreman and Naomi, mostly talk. Ruth says little and acts all the more: she goes, arrives, gleans, falls on her face and bows herself to the earth before Boaz, goes to sit with the gleaners, eats with them, has something left, gets up again, gleans again, extracts the ears, takes the grain and goes to Bethlehem with it, gives it to Naomi, tells her everything and again attaches herself to Boaz's young women and remains gathering ears until the end of the two harvests. She is almost exhaustingly active. But just as Ruth's courage has its humble side, so alongside all her activities we can see a certain passivity. Really passivity is not the right word. Ruth is aware of her dependence on others. She herself calls it 'finding grace in someone's eyes'. There is no doubt that for her the grace of someone on whom one is dependent counts more than all her own actions. Therefore she herself mentions this grace three times, in vv.3, 10 and 13.

To us nowadays the word 'grace' sounds somewhat strange. If someone is wrestling with a difficult problem and is told 'Just rely on God's grace', this grace is being used to cover up all kinds of incomprehensible things and provide a nice warmth. Even in modern views of grace as 'a gift of God and a task for human beings', sometimes the unctious voice still comes through loudly. However, in interviews with athletes you can hear something that might be called a modern version of grace. You often hear top athletes saying that with all the training in the world one cannot force success; there is something more. It is striking that the very people who devote so much to their sport and adapt their whole life-style to it say that they wouldn't get far without that surplus. It might almost be said that it is precisely because they have trained so hard and done everything they can that they can see more clearly that not everything is in their own hands. Of course they would never win unless they did all that they could. The surplus cannot be reduced to self-discipline or talent: it presupposes all the effort and builds on it, but one can't count on the effort. I would want to call this surplus the sporting version of grace.

Any form of grace is irritating and irrational: 'Why do you have that extra and I don't, when I've practised just as hard on the violin?' Why do you have more talent than I do?' In any life, from birth, at which one person gets more talent than another, through upbringing and teaching, to a career, isn't there a great difference in good fortune, in the distribution of qualities? Is it really fair that Carl Lewis can run so fast and I can't? Perhaps he doesn't write as well. Grace has nothing to do with a just distribution of qualities all round. Grace isn't deserved, yet it is received. We can't refer to our right to grace; that right is primarily taken out of our hands.

Ruth also works hard: not to be a champion athlete, but to survive. Just because she does so much, she recognizes the great value of the undeserved extra. And here undeserved doesn't mean that she hasn't earned it, but that no one is obligated to her for anything. Because for her the question is one of survival, she is dependent on that surplus. However hard the efforts that she makes, she cannot get any further unless someone notices her. She is aware of that, which is why she puts so much emphasis on 'finding grace in someone's eyes'. It is other people's eyes that count, since someone has to notice her if this encounter is going to happen. However, this other has no obligations to her. She cannot appeal to any law; she can only ask and wait. The powerlessness of someone who is dependent on the grace of another can be read off her long wait in the field. Hour after hour she waits for an answer: patiently, but without any certainty about the outcome. If she isn't given permission, then starvation faces her and Naomi. For her, grace is not a entirely free: she can do nothing without it, and yet she can do nothing to get it.

Going and waiting, courage and humility, acting and hoping for grace, pursuing ideals and acting realistically – here Ruth shows us all these things at the same time. She is no angel; the bare necessities of life compel her to be inventive. We are rather feeble compared with her. Our circumstances are less grim, but Ruth's behaviour can be inspiring, particularly if we see it at a more universal level. To make that clear we shall make a detour through two very different intermezzi and then return to Ruth.

Intermezzo 1

In September 1992, Tamarah Benima gave the third Abel Herzberg lecture which was printed in the journal Trouw. *Here are some short fragments for it.*

A sheep. A sheep is an impossibly stupid animal, but nevertheless it is not easy to catch. I was not the only one who had been ordered to catch a sheep; we were with a group. The sheep were running around in a great meadow on a hill, with a hedge around it. Individual action was no use. If you got near the flock, it immediately ran away. So a group strategy had to be devised and put into practice. That worked. At a given moment we had driven the flock into one corner of the land and slowly, slowly, we were able to get so close that it actually became possible to catch a sheep. In other words, slowly the moment approached when I, like my fellow sheep-catchers, had to go over to another form of action. As long as we were engaged in the approach, I was mentally preoccupied with strategy: shall I take a step to the left or to the right, must I go more slowly or more quickly? The physical activity and the mental activity went on side by side. But a moment came which was different, a moment when pure action was needed, now. The next moment I had got the sheep firmly in my grasp. Shortly before that moment of pure action started, there was a kind of anxiety, a moment of restraint; I had to go through it before I could plunge into the unknown. I overcame the 'anxiety' and threw myself confidently into the action.

Later my spiritual director sent me out again. Now it was to look for a partner. This was a 'task' for which I showed considerably less enthusiasm than for catching the sheep, but I set to work at it, because of course it touched a chord. But where was I to find a man? The only thing that I did was to work or drive a car to and from my work. Well, first Providence made

*my car break down and I had to go by train. And lo and behold,
there was a man in the train. But, as these things happen, before
I knew it, he had already got off the train and was on his way. I
cursed myself. I had a year of spiritual training behind me, just
to prepare me for situations in which action had to be taken,
but the moment such a situation came up I couldn't deal with it.
As so often happens. Angrily I spent two days at the key
moment waiting at the station where the man had got out.
There were two possibilities: either my beloved passenger had
been sitting in the train by chance and wouldn't appear at that
station again, or he had a fixed journey and took the same
commuter train every day at more or less the same time and got
out at the station at more or less the same time. It was fearfully
cold, and I stood freezing for hours. No man. God's ways are
unfathomable, so there was the possibility that Providence
would attach me to another man. But that didn't prove to be the
case. I saw tens of thousands of English go by, each one uglier
than the one before, tired, sour, unattractive, grim, grey, no one
even worth noticing. But when the chance had become minimal,
there was my beloved passenger, on a platform a long way off. I
rushed over to it; he got into the train and so did I. I proved to
have ten minutes to consider what I wanted. The man got out of
the train, I got out of the train, and then again came the same
sort of moment as in catching the sheep; a moment came when I
really had to act, and take a step into the dark. Step, step, step,
the distance between us got less, I came closer, now . . . caught.
Thank God I was treated to a surprised smile, and quite a
happy ending.*

*Anyone who looks at their own behaviour carefully will note
that this kind of crucial moment occurs frequently in life, a
moment when you have to act without knowing what the outcome will be. The first step when a child begins to walk is such
a moment, or cycling away for the first time with no one holding your bicycle, saying yes in a marriage ceremony, becoming
pregnant, making someone pregnant, taking up a career, leaving
home to begin a new life somewhere else, forgiving someone,
and so on. However much you plan, think it out, reflect,
arrange things, there comes a moment, now. And many people
don't get to lead lives of their own, not because they don't know*

what they want, but because they can't take this one step, where literally blind trust is needed.'

Intermezzo 2

In November 1992 Vaclav Havel gave a speech on the occasion of his installation as a member of the French 'Académie des sciences morales et politiques', a translation of which was printed in Trouw. *Here is part (a great deal) of this speech.*

'There are several ways of waiting. "Waiting for Godot" as an embodiment of redemption or universal salvation is one extreme on the broad scale on which different forms of waiting can be set. The waiting of many of us – those of us who lived under Communism – was often, or even constantly, up against this limit. Surrounded, shut in, colonized from within by a totalitarian system, people lost any hope of a way out, the will to act, indeed even the feeling that they could act. In short, they lost all hope. And yet they did not lose the need for a certain expectation; they could not lose this, since without hope life loses its meaning. Therefore they waited for Godot. When there was no hope to buoy them up within, they expected it from a vague salvation from outside. But Godot – the one who is waited for – never comes, simply because he does not exist. He is only a surrogate of hope. Summoned up by our powerlessness, he does not embody hope, but an illusion. He is a bandage for the bleeding or to bind up a broken heart, even if it is full of holes. This is the waiting of people without hope.

At the opposite end of the scale we find a different kind of waiting: waiting as the practice of patience. This is a waiting which is fed by the belief that to offer opposition by speaking the truth is a matter of principle; something that one simply has to do, without calculating whether this commitment will ever bear fruit, tomorrow or later, or whether it will just remain empty. It is a waiting that is strong in this conviction without concerning itself with the question of what weight this rebel truth puts in the scale, without knowing whether it will ever triumph or whether – as so often – it will be stifled. It is also, but only secondarily, a waiting that is supported by the conviction that the grain which has been sown will one day send

*out roots and germinate. No one knows when. Ever. Perhaps
for other generations. This attitude which – to put it simply –
we call dissidence presupposes patience and cultivates it. It has
taught us to be patient and to wait. This is waiting as exercising
patience, as a state of expectation, not as an expression of
despair. Waiting for Godot is meaningless: in doing so we make
fools of ourselves and only waste our time. But this other way
of waiting does make sense. Waiting for the grain of corn to
germinate is good in principle; it's different form 'waiting for
Godot'. Waiting for Godot means waiting for the blossoming of
a lily that we have never planted.*

*Let me speak for myself. Although I was practised in this
capacity to wait patiently, which is characteristic of dissidents,
and convinced of its deeper meaning, in the last three years, i.e.
after the peaceful anti-totalitarian revolution, I sank deeper and
deeper into an impatience bordering on despair. I tormented
myself with the thought that the changes were going far too
slowly, that my country still did not have a new democratic
basic law, that the Czechs and the Slovaks no longer knew how
to co-exist within one state, that we were not growing quickly
enough towards the Western democratic world and its struc-
tures, that we could not assimilate the past in a meaningful way,
that the remains of the former government and its moral wilder-
ness were being removed too slowly. With the courage of
despair I hoped to be able to achieve at least one of these goals,
in order to be able to cross off one problem as having been
solved. I wanted the work that I was doing as head of the
country finally to culminate in a visible, irrefutable, tangible and
undeniable result, a real achievement. I found it difficult to get
into my head the idea that politics, like history, is an endless
process, a process in which nothing can finally be finished,
rounded off and said to be ended. It was as if I had simply
forgotten to wait, to wait in the only meaningful way.*

*Now that I'm distanced from all that, I've plenty of time to
think about it again. And I'm beginning to understand that I
let my impatience lead me astray into precisely what I had
always analysed so critically. I was led astray by the devastating
impatience of modern technocratic civilization, full as it is of its
own rationality, and wrongly convinced that the world is no*

*more than a crossword puzzle with just one correct – so-called
objective – solution: a solution the outcome of which only I can
determine. In short, I thought that I was lord and master of
time. That was a great mistake. I noted with dismay that my
impatience over the restoration of democracy had a rationalistic
element to it. I wanted to make history progress like a child
going to tear a plant to make it grow faster. I believe that we
have to learn to wait as we learn to create. We must patiently
sow the seeds of grain, water the earth in which they are sown
and give the plants time. There is no reason to be impatient if
the sowing and the watering is good. It is enough for us to see
that it is not senseless to wait. Waiting makes sense because it is
fed by hope and not by despair, by trust and not by hopelessness, by humility towards the time of this world and not by fear,
does not lead to boredom but is full of excitement. Such expectation is more than just waiting.'*

Pure action and patience

Ruth does not have to catch either a sheep or a partner, though
the latter is not completely clear. Ruth does not need to be head
of a government or a political dissident. But the properties
which Benima and Havel have described, each in their distinctive ways, are characteristic of her. Ruth is more than once
aware of the choice of H-Hour as Benima describes it. At that
moment of action she takes the plunge and goes. In the first part
of the story there was such a moment of pure action when she
decided to go with Naomi to Bethlehem. Her sister-in-law and
kinswoman Orpah turns round and goes back. Then Ruth has
to choose: whether to go back with the one to Moab, or to
go away with the other to a foreign land. She turns away from
her homeland and goes to meet the unknown future. There is
another such moment in the second chapter. Ruth has only just
arrived in Bethlehem when she goes into the fields and there
takes the plunge: she boldly asks the foreman to be allowed to
gather ears near the sheaves. Things could have gone badly for
her, but she takes the risk.

Besides this, Ruth is also Havel's waiting dissident. She is
rowing against the current. She is a dissident because she differs

from the rest; she sows her own seed and waits for the harvest.
She waits patiently. She has put her bold question and knows
that she is dependent on the good will of others. She senses that
however enterprising she is, she cannot programme everything.
She has made her own contribution, and now it has to
come from others. This is no waiting for Godot, but a hopeful
waiting. Of course it would be wrong to suggest that Ruth is a
great philosopher or theologian, a thinker of the stature of
Havel. She is more a woman of action than one of words. But
these actions are based on faith, trust and ideals.

In her faith and ideals Ruth differs from Naomi and Boaz.
Naomi's earlier wish had been that YHWH would do good to her
daughter-in-law, because she had done good to her, Naomi.
Moreover she indicated that she was disappointed in YHWH
because he had abandoned her and plunged her into misery. She
firmly and constantly believed in a good order, in a balance
between action and reward, and in the form of social life
handed down and regulated from antiquity: the organizations
of her own family, her own clan, her own tribe, her own
religion and her own God. She wanted her daughters-in-law to
find rest in their own land and home, with their own (Moabite)
husband and their own God. To find rest, *masa menucha
(m.n.ch)*, to find stability, that was and is her ideal. Over against
this Ruth sets her own ideal: she goes, she commits herself, and
this commitment to the dead and to Naomi and the risk that she
takes determine her life. She does not strive for rest but hopes to
find grace: *masa chen (ch.n)*. Ruth is not concerned about what
falls within a predetermined order or what belongs to the law,
but about the plus factor. That is the extra that cannot be calcu-
lated, that sometimes happens to one unexpectedly. But the way
in which one deals with the unexpected can differ: one can
expect nothing and do nothing, or one can first sow and then
wait patiently and full of trust. But things can always go wrong.
Ruth and her mother-in-law can die of hunger. Naomi can
drag her into her defeatism. She can become a sour, lonely old
woman. But she clings on to all the bits of hope and uses all the
possibilities that they offer to realize her ideal.

Boaz resembles Naomi in his ideals. Although he appreciates
the unusual thing that Ruth has done, he continues to believe in

his own ideal: a balanced society ordered in accordance with the insights of his own group and his own God. He indicates that with the word *shalem*, which is closely connected with *shalom*. These words indicate the order, the regularity, on which people can reckon. Such regularity is needed to create security and order in a culture and society. From this perspective Boaz hopes that YHWH will reward Ruth and that his recompense will be as great as her efforts. He wants YHWH to behave in a way which corresponds to Ruth's behaviour. He also does his bit by being friendly and accommodating to Ruth and doing more than he really needs to. Ruth has adopted the faith of Judah and is very grateful to him for his good will. But Ruth is no stupid sheep; she has her own courage and her own cunning. Thus in Chapter 1 she can turn Naomi's request for her to go away into a request not to abandon Naomi. And here she dares to ask the foreman for something that is on the limit of the permissible. But her behaviour in the next chapter exceeds everything. To go and lie at a man's feet on the threshing floor at midnight is not only bold, but even deadly dangerous. Here Ruth is putting her life as an honest woman at stake. Compared with that, Benima's hunt for the man on the train is nothing.

A foreigner seen

Ruth is aware that she is a foreigner. Once, in v.10, she shows that for her there is a connection between finding grace in someone's eyes and her being a foreigner:

2.10b   She said to him,
         'Why do I find grace in your eyes,
         that you should take notice of me,
         when I am a foreigner?'

A term frequently used for foreigner in the Hebrew Bible is *ger*. Ruth uses another Hebrew word, *nochria*, from the verb *nachar*, 'see', a literal translation of which is 'someone who is seen' or 'the one seen'. Thus a foreigner is someone who is seen, and is seen because he or she strikes people as strange, as different from the indigenous population. So the foreman

immediately sees that Ruth is a Moabitess, just as we see someone walking along and know that they are, say, Pakistani. In
England, English people don't stand out, but abroad you can
pick them out easily. Thus to perceive often means to see what
is other about something or someone, since it is the difference
that makes perception possible. Here it is the one who looks
and not the person perceived who gives direction to this gaze.
Now it is striking that Ruth describes herself with a word which
belongs to the perspective of the indigenous person, as 'the one
who is seen'. She knows that she is dependent on the gaze of the
one who sees. In so doing she puts herself at risk as an independent person. This ambiguity characterizes Ruth. She does a lot:
she resolves even to go away from her people to Judah; she
resolves to go to the field. She is thus autonomous, yet at the
same time she knows that she is dependent on the eyes of someone who sees her as being other. You can do so much, but it is
impossible to direct the eyes of someone elsewhere. In this sense
Ruth is right when she calls that 'grace'. She cannot direct the
well-wishing eyes of others.

The people of Judah, from whose perspective this story has
been written, are not dependent on the gaze of others and
certainly not on that of Ruth. They form the majority and
are not foreigners. Ruth belongs to a foreign minority and is
encapsulated in their world. To recognize the otherness of
others does not mean to think them valuable. Ruth is the only
one to use the term grace. She knows that other people and God
are not dependent on her gaze. She is fully aware that she is
dependent both on the other people who see her, and on God
who looks after her. In the case of Naomi and Boaz, things seem
to be rather different: they think of God as other and thus make
God dependent on their gaze. Sooner or later it emerges that
God is not dependent on their gaze, but that they are dependent
on his. They could learn that from Ruth. But whether they
actually do so is to be doubted, for the book is and remains
written from a particular order and perspective, which is that of
Judah.

In Ruth's own words

How burning hot the sun is! I can feel the rays piercing me. It's lucky I have a headscarf on. My hair underneath is wet through, it's so boiling under the scarf. It's hard, even harder than I'd expected. Sometimes I feel so dizzy that the world begins to go round and round before my eyes. Once I even fell over. Fortunately no one noticed; everyone is so desperately busy. Sometimes when I'm afraid that it's going to happen again, I stand up straight. If the dizziness doesn't go away and a wave of sickness passes over me, I go right next to the jars with water in to drink a cup of water. My, how marvellously refreshing the water is then! Back at my nice place just behind the reapers things go well after that. As long as it lasts.

If you're standing hour after hour in the fields you've a lot of time to reflect. You keep thinking about things while your hands are looking for grains of barley. Certainly at the beginning of the day I reflect a great deal. Later, your gaze gets fixed. And finally you only think of water, Water, WATER. But before it gets that far I go back in my mind to Moab, the land of my birth. After my marriage I became increasingly detached from my family, my land and religion. But now that I'm here, I miss it. I think of the songs we used to sing, of the merriment. Naomi hasn't been merry for a long time; the people here are more serious. For them life is a task, and I miss my husband, Mahlon. He was a quiet man. Outsiders thought that he and his brother Chilion were twins, they were so like each other. But I could see the difference. Now neither of them is here any more. My father-in-law had already died earlier. With all these dead people around me, I sometimes feel an old woman. Naomi has lost her husband and both sons. So she has a much heavier burden to bear. I mustn't complain.

That gleaning is a business that requires a great deal of patience. All day, hour in hour out, bending, turning, looking, waiting, and now and then finding something. However, the only thing that matters is that we, Naomi and I, don't perish of hunger. But I don't know how we're going to get on for the rest of the year if there isn't another harvest. I know that it would be difficult. When I opted in Moab for Judah, YHWH and Naomi,

and through them for my dead husband, I did so with great con-
viction. But the crazy thing is that at the moment when you
choose, you don't realize what you're leaving behind and where
you're going. Here in Judah many people think that they own
the truth. Not Boaz, he's a wise man. But others do. And they
simply can't bear criticism. 'Only people who belong to our
group can criticize us,' they say. 'Others don't understand any-
thing about us; they must keep to themselves.' In my view this
only leads to navel-gazing. Suppose that everyone only looked
at their own group and their own part of history. In that case, in
Moab I wouldn't have heard of Judah and Elimelek, and Naomi
wouldn't have known about Moab. We Moabites have also
experienced much: war, devastation and torture, famine, but
we're open to others. We don't claim that our misery was the
greatest misery, that our prosperity was the greatest prosperity,
that our God is the only God. Things are different here in
Judah. Their own history is the only one that counts. Sometimes
someone tries to defend the exclusive attention to their own
group with the term election. But authoritative men in the gate
have rejected that: 'Election gives us obligations to others and
doesn't give us the right to slap ourselves on our backs,' they
said. And I agree with them. Not that my view is asked for,
since of course people don't ask women about anything.

People here in Judah forget that I first lived in another culture
and religion and that therefore I can make comparisons better
than they can. I now realize how much the Moabite culture and
religion in which I grew up was and is tied to the time and place
and the people there. At the same time I see the same thing in
Bethlehem: this religion and culture, too, is bound to this place,
to these people and their history, to their perspective. And I
notice that they, like most people in Moab, regard their way of
looking at things as normative and all-decisive. They are well
aware that their perspective and faith is tied only to Israel and
that their God is the God of Israel, but at the same time they
make this God a universal God and call their laws God's laws,
the basic law for all human beings. Just imagine all those
peoples in the world who all have their own views and who all
think that God shares their perspective! How dizzy God would
get, even dizzier than me standing in the field in the sun!

It may be that I've lost the thread. Now and then I have that feeling. I no longer really know who I am. Sometimes I think and dream in Moabite, and then again in Hebrew, the language of Judah. Sometimes I feel one with the family and clan of Elimelek, and then again I think, 'What am I doing here?' It's a kind of knot in myself. It's as if the whole problem of intercultural relations was being fought out in me. My stomach and guts join in the fight. It's confusing and yet it's gradually beginning to dawn on me. At least that's what I think. I shall never be able to think in such absolute terms that everything depends simply on my history and life story; I shall never again be able to escape the insight that everything is connected with the perspective of the person who is looking. I know what it's like to stand with empty hands or to be ground between two cultures. The only thing that still counts in my eyes is responsible action: doing the truth. Although there is no absolute and eternally valid truth, what is good here and now for particular people and in accord with their ideals is true or worthwhile. I've made my choice for Naomi and the dead. There my commitment lies, and that's what I shall dedicate myself to in what I do.

I feel torn apart. I know that the others don't depend on my eyes, and YHWH, *the God of Israel, certainly does not depend on me. On the other hand I feel that as a foreigner I myself am dependent on those who notice me. Their eyes can make me or break me. They can cast me into the abyss, and make me feel the emptiness of existence. I'm nothing without them.*

Ruth 3: Midnight

1a Naomi her mother-in-law said to her,

1b 'My daughter, shall I not seek for you a rest
which will be good for you?

2a And now, is not Boaz our kinsman,
the one with whose young women you have been?

2b Look, he is going to winnow barley on the threshing floor
tonight.

3a Bathe yourself,
anoint yourself,
put on your best clothes,
and go down to the threshing floor.

3b Do not make yourself known to the man
until he has finished his eating and drinking.

4a When he goes to lie down,
note the place
where he lies.
Then go close,
take your clothes off at the place by his feet
and lie down.

4b And he will tell you
what you must do.'

5a She said to her,

5b 'All that you have said,
I will do.'

6a So she went down to the threshing floor

6b and she did just as her mother-in-law had commanded.

7a Boaz ate
and drank,
and his heart was good.
He went to lie down at the end of the heap of grain.

7b She came secretly,
and took off her clothes at the place by his feet
and lay down.

8a Around midnight it happened

that the man woke up startled,
turned over

8b   and behold there was a woman lying at the place by his feet.

9a   He said,
> 'Who are you?'

9b   She said,
> 'I am Ruth your maidservant.
> Spread your wings/cloak over your maidservant,
> for you are a redeemer.'

10a   He said,
> 'Blessed are you by YHWH, my daughter,
> for with this goodness you have surpassed the former.

10b
> You have not gone after the young men
> whether poor or rich.

11a
> Now, my daughter, do not be afraid.
> All that you have said,
> I will do for you.

11b
> For all the people at the gate know
> that you are a strong woman.

12a
> Now it is indeed true that I am a redeemer,

12b
> yet there is also a redeemer
> who is more closely related than I am.

13a
> Remain here for the night,
> and in the morning, if he will redeem you
> good, let him redeem you.
> If he is not willling to redeem you,
> I will redeem you,
> as truly as YHWH lives.

13b
> So lie here until the morning.'

14a   And she lay at the place by his feet until the morning.
She got up
before a man could see his neighbour.

14b   He said,
> 'No one must know
> that the woman came to the threshing floor.'

15a   He said,
> 'Give me the shawl
> that is on you
> and hold it out.'

She held it

15b   and he measured out six measures of barley
and laid it upon her.

He went to the city.

16a She came to her mother-in-law
and she said,
'Who are you, my daughter?'

16b And she told her
all that the man had done for her.

17a She said,
'These six measures of barley he gave to me,

17b for, he said,
you must not go back empty-handed to your mother-in-law.'

18a She said,
'Wait, my daughter,
until you know
how the matter turns out.

18b The man will not rest
until he settles the matter today.'

Through Naomi's eyes

Naomi's initiative

The harvest is over and for the moment Ruth and Naomi have enough grain to bake bread. But how are things to go on? Because during the harvest Ruth has been only with young women and not with young men, she has not been in a position to meet a possible spouse. And now she is sitting at home again, she no longer has any opportunity to see Boaz or other men. Certainly, Ruth has opted for her mother-in-law, but unless she does something else, in the end death by starvation threatens both of them. As a foreigner there is no question of her being considered for a marriage with a member of the family which has obligations towards her dead husband. The marriage rules serve to protect one's own group, and foreigners do not belong to it. Boaz has already behaved admirably as a relative. He helped Ruth far more than he need have done and saw to it that she got enough grain. She cannot reasonably expect more.

Now finally a real solution must be sought. Naomi begins to talk: 'My daughter, shall I not seek for you a rest which will be good for you?' (3.1). Naomi is out for a definitive solution. She wants a solid and quiet place for Ruth. The word 'rest' or 'resting place' is a literal translation of the Hebrew, but for us it conjures up too much the picture of 'eternal rest'. Something less permanent would be better. Already earlier, in 1.9, Naomi had expressed the wish that 'Orpah and Ruth should find (a) rest(ing place), a woman in the house of her husband'. In her view, rest can only be found in certain places, and for a woman that is in the house of a husband. Earlier Naomi expressed a wish for such a place to Ruth and hoped that YHWH would help her. She herself did nothing to speed it on. Now she says that she herself will look for such a place or home for her. A resting place evidently does not seem to be just there for the taking. For rest you have to do something, make rest for yourself. Naomi now tries herself to achieve what she had first left to YHWH in a wish that was also a prayer.

Naomi the stage-manager

Naomi has devised a plan and makes Ruth an accomplice in it: 'Boaz is our kinsman. You know him, because you've worked with his young women. Tonight he's on the threshing floor.' Boaz is not just 'a kinsman of Elimelek', as the narrator said in 2.1, nor is he just 'near to us', as Naomi informed Ruth earlier in 2.20. Now Naomi describes him in 3.2 as 'a kinsman of ours'. Boaz is coming steadily closer in her perspective, since in her eyes he has also become Ruth's family. She is planning something for this man and Ruth. They already know each other from the field. Now they are to know each other on the threshing floor by night. In the ancient Near East the threshing floor was regularly associated with fertility; so something can be going to happen here.

Naomi unfolds the scene. In a few rapid and staccato sentences she urges Ruth on: 'Bathe yourself, anoint yourself, put on your clothes, go down, go close, take your clothes off, go and lie down.' Most mothers(-in-law) give their daughters(-in-law) different advice. At the heart of the series of actions stands the verb 'know' (*yada*): 'don't make yourself known to the man who is known to us, but know well the place where he lies'. There has to be a difference in knowledge between Boaz and Ruth: she knows Boaz's identity, but he doesn't know hers; she knows where he is lying, but he is not aware of her presence.

The veil of darkness by night brings about the opposite of knowing. And at the same time it makes this night a possibility for (sexual) knowing, for an unveiling knowing. So knowledge and secrecy strive for the upper hand on this night.

As in a play or film, everything turns on the right time and the right place. Naomi's plan also turns on that. The effect would be lost if these things don't work out. Moreover Naomi three times uses the term 'place': a resting place, the place where Boaz goes to lie, and the place at his feet. The exact place and the precise moment of action are important. The time which Naomi hopes will be 'good' for Ruth is the time when Boaz will have eaten and drunk and things will be 'good' with him. Boaz's good resting place must become the good resting place for Ruth.

As readers, we immediately see how carefully the narrator has arranged the indications of time and place throughout the book of Ruth. The book begins with a very general indication of time, 'in the time of the judges', and this is gradually made increasingly precise. After the death of the three male members of the family we no longer hear about the time of the judges in general, but about one year and one period of harvest. Then the whole harvest season is concentrated into one night. And finally, it has to happen at a particular time during this night. In Chapter 4 the time will spread out again: the day dawns again, then there is the time of pregnancy, and gradually in the genealogy at the end of the book the time fans out to be quite broad. So the chronological structure in this book proves to have the form of an hour-glass. The same happens with the ordering of place. Beginning with Judah and Moab, the narrator goes on to direct our attention to Bethlehem and to the field near Bethlehem. Then the story concentrates on one place, the threshing floor. And finally the focus is the exact place on the threshing floor, the place at Boaz's feet. After that the space broadens out again: first the city gate comes into view, then Bethlehem, and finally all Israel. The setting is carefully constructed, from large to small and then to large again. In Chapter 3, as readers we find ourselves in the smallest space and at the most concentrated moment. Here the drama takes place in all its identity. If it does not happen here and now, it will never happen anywhere.

Naomi is too cunning for the law

To make something happen that really sinks in, in planning one has to know the rules which regulate or limit the action. To be able to see through the plan, the reader must know what Naomi knows, namely the nature of marriage legislation in Judah. For that is what her staging of 'H-Hour' on the threshing floor is based on. Suppose that a man dies and leaves his wife without children. In such a case, Jewish legislation makes provision for the name of the dead man to survive. To enable this, the brother of the dead husband (the brother-in-law or *levir*) must marry the widow and have sexual intercourse with her. This is called a levirate or brother-in-law's marriage. Sometimes such a marriage is connected with redemption and one person can perform two tasks: as redeemer he can see to it that the possessions are retained in the clan, and as *levir* he can marry the widow. If a son is born of this marriage, then the son is regarded as the dead man's son, who has to continue the name of the dead man in the clan possessions. If all the brothers of the dead man are dead, then the father is eligible for a levirate marriage with his daughter-in-law. If all the male offspring are dead, it is an unimaginable disaster. One of the worst things that can happen to a man is for him and his name not to live on. The levirate laws are aimed at preventing such a thing happening.

In the case of Naomi, her husband and sons are dead and she herself is too old to have children. Her daughter-in-law Ruth has lost her husband, brother-in-law and father-in-law, but for her there is the complication that she is a foreign woman, and moreover a Moabite. Israelite law says that Israelites may not marry Moabites, because that would dilute faith in YHWH and endanger the ongoing existence of the clan or tribe. The levirate laws did not recognize any obligations towards foreigners who had married into the family or clan. That is logical, for such a foreigner is not in a position to continue the name and the religion in her own group. Naomi grew up with this legislation and knows it well. Therefore she did not need Orpah and Ruth to go with her from Moab to Bethlehem. Naomi herself could not have more children, and any children which she and another husband from Judah might have would not be able to keep the dead man's name alive. According to Naomi it was completely senseless for Ruth nevertheless to go with her.

Gradually Naomi changes and opts for an alternative solution. She does two things. First of all she regards Ruth as a member of the family and Boaz as a redeemer of both herself and Ruth. Then she directs Ruth to the threshing floor. This is a bold attempt to be too cunning for the law. Only desperate people can try this sort of thing. They have had all other possibilities taken out of their hands. Tamar was a similar desperate case. Her story is told in Genesis 38. Tamar's husband had died and had left her no children. The brother who later had intercourse with her died suddenly without giving her a child. Then her father-in-law Judah refused to do his duty by the law. Finally Tamar disguised herself as a prostitute and went to sit with her head covered at the entrance to the city, waiting until Judah came. Judah had intercourse with the prostitute, not knowing that she was Tamar. When she bore a son, the whole story came out and Judah had to confess that he had not fulfilled his legal obligations and that Tamar was within her rights. The son born to her and Judah continued the name of her dead husband.

Since the law does not offer Ruth the possibility of providing descendants through a levirate marriage, Naomi thinks up a trick. It is a cunning plan which resembles Tamar's plan, but this time the person who devises the plan is not the one who carries it out. Naomi gives Ruth detailed instructions about the precise place and the right time where and when Ruth must take off her clothes, go and lie down, and wait. There are three actions here, the first active and the last two passive. The active one is of course the most decisive. This action is usually translated as 'uncover his feet', which is quite different from my translation 'take your clothes off at the place by his feet'. The Hebrew words are *gillit margelotaw*, of which *gillit* means 'she undresses' and *margelotaw* 'the place of the feet' ('feet' would have been *regel*). *margelotaw* is (as the prefix *ma* shows) the indication of a place, like for example 'the threshing floor' or 'in the city gate'. It cannot be the direct object of Ruth's unclothing activity, otherwise there would have been an object marker *et* in Hebrew; it is the place where she executes her action. So Ruth, at a certain place, namely the place where Boaz feet's are lying, has to uncover or undress someone. There are only two possible persons: Boaz or herself. In the option that Ruth undresses Boaz, the name of Boaz would have had to be mentioned as the one involved, and that is not the case. Perhaps it's a pity, but Ruth does not take Boaz's clothes off, otherwise he probably wouldn't have been sleeping so peacefully. The other option is that Ruth has to take her own clothes off. Actually, this is confirmed by the scene on the threshing floor, when Ruth asks Boaz, 'Spread your cloak over your maidservant'. She needs covering, Boaz doesn't. Thus, it is obvious from the Hebrew words and the context that Naomi tells Ruth to undress herself at the place at the feet of Boaz, and to lie down there. Deeply embarrassed, people have always ruled out this possibility. In the Christian tradition this problem is solved by saying that Ruth is told by Naomi to lie humbly at Boaz's feet and to uncover his feet. Thus this text becomes a symbol of Ruth's great humility. No one has dared to think of a striptease.

All the orders which Naomi gives relate to actions which Ruth must perform on herself. She must wash, anoint herself, go to the place, take her clothes off and lie down. Just as Tamar sought a clever way of attracting Judah's attention through her clothing, so Naomi seeks a good way for Ruth to attract Boaz's attention through her lack of clothing. Moreover the precise place, and waiting for the precise moment, are of enormous importance for both women. For Tamar this is the gate and Judah's coming; for Ruth it is the place where Boaz lies on the threshing floor. Totally naked, she lies waiting to see what Boaz is going to do. For that moment there are no actions or words for Ruth in the scenario. In Naomi's plan the words come only from Boaz, and Naomi cannot either prescribe or stage-manage them: 'He will tell you what you must do.' Ruth must first herself take an enormous risk and then wait to see what happens.

Naomi learns from Ruth

Naomi hears what happens on the threshing floor only long after the nocturnal events have taken place. It is early in the morning when Ruth returns home. Then Naomi puts the same question to her that Boaz had put earlier, 'Who are you?'. It seems a stupid question; surely she knows Ruth? Perhaps it was still too dark, and one woman couldn't distinguish another. But it is more probable that the narrator is here deliberately suggesting that Naomi is asking the same question as Boaz's first question. As older people they both react identically: they both address Ruth as 'my daughter' and begin 'Who are you?' and 'What do you want?' It is even possible that this question indicates that Naomi is cautiously testing whether Ruth has changed. In the meantime she could have become Boaz's wife. In this sense Naomi is asking about Ruth's identity. Just as Boaz asked who Ruth was, so Naomi is asking how Ruth now sees herself. Ruth tells Naomi what has happened. After that Naomi quickly takes the initiative and says, 'Wait until you know how the matter turns out' (3.18). In her view Ruth must wait patiently. No more toil or rushing; patience is now the watchword.

It is striking how much Naomi has learned from Ruth in a short time. In Chapter 1 we were looking through Naomi's eyes and feeling her discontent with everything. Her dearest wish was to return, and she didn't undertake anything else. She found nothing any good, and reacted in an embittered and sour way. Ruth did not; she blazed with energy; she went with Naomi, even though she didn't know what the future would bring. When she arrived in Bethlehem, she displayed the same pattern. Naomi did nothing and remained at home, whereas Ruth immediately went out into the field. A combination of activity and patient waiting characterized Ruth, both in Moab and in the field. Only when Ruth returned and Naomi showed her the basket full of grain and the handful of remnants from the midday meal did Naomi begin to thaw. Could there be a future for her after all? In this chapter we see how Naomi follows Ruth's example and no longer allows fate to run its course, but herself undertakes something. She devises a plan, one might almost say a war plan. The plan is not without risk and can go terribly wrong. Then the two of them will be sitting at home for the moment without much to eat. But, Naomi thinks, nothing venture, nothing win. She advises Ruth on a great many actions, with an equally large dose of patience, and argues for action

without forcing things. Naomi does what Ruth did in Chapters
1 and 2. She has learned from Ruth that she must not go on
hoping for providence to do something, but can take the initiative herself. Once you've undertaken something, you can only
trust that other people will make their contribution. And then
wait.

Ruth generally has the reputation of being a convert. She was
a Moabite who believed in Chemosh the God of the Moabites,
and she became a believer in YHWH. She abandons her people,
her land and her God in order to embrace Naomi's people and
the God of Israel. She is a foreigner who in the eyes of the
indigenous believers in YHWH is a newcomer and an outsider.
And now Naomi learns from her and her view of YHWH.
Through the trust that Ruth instils in her, the unconditional
option for her and her belief, and above all Ruth's good example, Naomi changes and begins to see that YHWH does not solve
all the problems for her. At first attached to the familiar order,
the law and the rules, Naomi is now ready to look for the seamy
side of the law and the opposite of the familiar order. Granted,
the risk that she runs is not as great as Ruth's; in the end of the
day, Ruth is the one who is lying on the threshing floor, and not
Naomi. And yet, if conversion is a radical change of perspective,
in this book not only Ruth but also Naomi is a convert. As an
indigenous woman of Judah who believes in YHWH, she learns
from the faith of a foreigner, and has her faith corrected by that
of Ruth. If Ruth first went with Naomi, now Naomi is following
Ruth's good example.

In Naomi's own words

*I don't know myself. I feel so much more cheerful recently.
When I look back a couple of months, to when I left Moab and
returned to Bethlehem, I realize just how desperate I was then. I
saw no way out. It was all too much for me. I had even finished
with YHWH. I felt so abandoned by everyone that I didn't even
notice Ruth.*

*Sometimes children, even children by marriage, are a bless-
ing. I was older and thought I knew the ways of the world. I
had been brought up in a fixed order and a faith which was pre-*

scribed exactly, and I thought that these were immovable and unchangeable. I and many others imposed this order on everything and everyone. But children are young and look at things differently. I noticed how my sons changed in Moab and that I couldn't follow them. Now and then I felt terribly alone, in such a strange land where everyone spoke a language that was foreign to me. There was no one who understood me. And then even your children grow away from you. It was difficult. When they died, I wanted to go back to Judah, to my own familiar world, to the people of my youth, to the faith of my ancestors. But when I got back I found that I'd changed. I was embittered as a result of everything that had happened to me. I couldn't take it when the women still called me 'lovely' as before, whereas I was no longer the same person. I thought that I had returned to the safe bosom of my people, but it was no longer so familiar and safe. I began to see the relativity in everything. I saw that even the order of Judah is based on customs and regulations which have been made and learned by human beings.

In retrospect I have to say that above all, the disillusionment at what had happened to me and anxiety for the future shaped my behaviour. Fortunately there are some people around you who can break through when you're completely shut up in yourself. Sometimes a child that looks at everyone with open eyes as if something nice, interesting or pleasant is going to happen can have such a cleansing influence. Ruth's behaviour had that effect on me. She's taught me a lot with her open attitude, the way that she gazes at the world full of trust, without being naive. I've so to speak borrowed her eyes, and I've begun to see that the world need not necessarily look the way I thought it looked.

So I thought that my trust in YHWH's *action with the world and my faith in his providence was a good faith. Moreover who knew who* YHWH *was, Ruth or I? Surely I'd been a believer in* YHWH *for ages and she hadn't? That, at least, is what I thought then. Gradually I've begun to see things differently. I've not abandoned my old faith; I continue to believe in* YHWH *as the one true God. But I no longer think that we people in Judah have a monopoly of the truth, that everything that we think about God is the only possible thing that you can think about*

God. Or that our – or rather, let me speak for myself, my – picture of God is the picture of God. I used to think that there was only one way to God, but now I see that one's picture of God depends on the course one takes. Otherwise God wouldn't be a living God for us, but a package accepted by our ancestors and handed down by them: God as a baton in a relay race. Now I would call God a 'companion', someone who goes with you on the way. That of course means that you yourself have to go on the way, otherwise God can't go with you. I've learned that from Ruth. She went on the way with me, even where there was no way. She made a way for both of us. Now in turn I've covered part of the course. How is that possible for me, the one who used to believe that faith in God's providence meant that one had to surrender oneself to everything, that one only needed to wait for providence to take the initiative? As if God hadn't given people hands and feet, understanding and ideas? As if when the sun shines I may not go and sit in the shadow, and if there is the threat of an infectious disease I may not go and get inoculated? I thought that that was faith. But I was wrong. You can learn from your own children and also from your children by marriage. You can even learn from a Moabite or a Somali. Or perhaps I have to say that you can learn particularly from them, because with their 'strange' ideas they can hold up a mirror to you which shows you what is absurd about your own view and behaviour.

Through Ruth's eyes

Ruth learns from Naomi

'All that you have said, I will do' is Ruth's reaction in v.5 to Naomi's plan and promptings, and following Naomi's advice she takes the way down to the threshing floor. Bethlehem lies on hills, and the floor where threshing and winnowing was done, i.e. a place where the grains of corn were beaten out of the ears and the wheat was separated from the chaff, would lie in a clearing or in a valley not far away. So this threshing and winnowing floor lay lower than Bethlehem, in a place where there was enough wind to winnow the grain. When Ruth has arrived at this threshing place, the narrator gets ahead of events in saying, 'she did all that her mother-in-law had commanded' (3.6b). It is clear: Ruth does what Naomi had devised earlier. It is characteristic that the narrator here uses the word 'command', where Ruth herself had been talking about what Naomi had 'said'. In Ruth's own words it sounds more as if she concurs, whereas the narrator brings out above all Naomi's role as instigator. Then he describes Ruth's actions in literally the same words as those used by Naomi. After Boaz has eaten and lain down, we read: 'She came secretly, and took off her clothes in the place by his feet and lay down' (3.7).

After that nothing happens. The narrator leaves a gap in time to show that after Ruth has gone to lie down she does not do anything else. Naomi had also commanded her to do that. Only when Boaz wakes up suddenly towards midnight does something happen. Up till then Ruth lies quietly there naked, waiting. It cannot have been easy; hopefully it was not too cold a night on the threshing floor. There she lies, small beneath the immeasurable starry heaven: at the feet of a man who is lying at the foot of a pile of grain, on a threshing floor in a valley. A woman in the dark night, surrendering to what is going to happen.

Midnight

Around midnight the man wakes up startled. Now it's going to happen. Naomi's words no longer have any role; Ruth has to go with the course of events. Contrary to Naomi's expectations, Boaz does not react with a command but with a question, 'Who are you?' (3.9a), and she replies,

3.9b   'I am Ruth your maidservant.
        Spread your wings/cloak over your maidservant,
        for you are a redeemer.'

Ruth lies naked at Boaz's feet and gives this subtly constructed reply. First she identifies herself. Then she doesn't wait for what Boaz tells her to do, as Naomi had commanded, but confronts Boaz with an urgent request.

First of all Ruth describes herself as a maidservant of Boaz and thus refers back to what she had said in the conversation with him in the field. There she first of all called herself a foreigner (2.10), in other words someone who stood outside the social and cultural group of Judah; later she says that she is someone who is not on the same level as one of Boaz's servants, and goes on to call herself Boaz's slave (2.13), i.e. someone who is on the lowest rung of the social ladder. By contrast, here on the threshing floor she speaks of herself not as a slave but as a woman servant. So we see in Ruth's own words the growth reflected by the picture of herself that she presents: from being an outsider and not even a slave, she sees herself as Boaz's slave and finally as his servant.

At the same time Ruth couples a command with this identification, and deliberately relates it to what Boaz had said to her in the field. Then he said:

2.12   'May YHWH recompense your work.
       May a full reward be paid to you
       by YHWH the God of Israel,
       to whom you have come
       to find refuge under his wings.'

Ruth uses the word 'wings', which Boaz also used, only it is not under YHWH's wings but under Boaz's wings that she seeks protection. By using the same word, Ruth shows that Boaz cannot hide behind YHWH's wings, but that he must spread out his own. Like Naomi, Boaz shifted his responsibility on to YHWH. Through Ruth's behaviour, Naomi has become convinced that she must do something herself and not foist everything on YHWH. And here Ruth tries to make it clear to Boaz that it is his turn to take the initiative. Moreover the word *kanaf*, wing, that she uses, has a double meaning: it means not only wing but also '(a point of the) cloak'. So with this word Ruth is referring not only to YHWH's wings but also to the custom (at that time) that a man who spread his cloak over a woman indicated that he took her as his wife. In a time when there were no registrars and no documents to establish certain matters, there were particular gestures or actions by which people endorsed agreements. Spreading out a garment or cloak symbolized contracting a marriage, and taking off a sandal symbolized the settling of a deal.

What can Boaz do after such a request? He can have intercourse with Ruth and then she becomes his wife. He can also spread his cloak over her, but this means the same thing in a symbolic way. In that case she will similarly become his wife. Thus for example we read in Ezekiel 16.8 that God sees Jerusalem lying as a naked woman: he takes his cloak and spreads it over her and thus indicates that he takes Jerusalem as his wife. Now we can see the full extent of Ruth's shrewdness, one might almost say her cunning. She lies there naked on the threshing floor and with her conversation puts Boaz on the spot: either he spreads his cloak over her and then she is his wife, or he has intercourse with her and then she has also become his wife. The only other possibility is for him to deny her nakedness and send here away, but that too requires courage. Just as Tamar seduced Judah by her clothing and afterwards confronted him with the consequences, so here Ruth is forcing Boaz to make a choice by her lack of clothing and her request. It is one or the other. Perhaps this is just what a foreigner does: confronts one with the other in all her or his nakedness and shows one that one has to make a choice.

And so on her way as an alien, via being Boaz's slave and servant, Ruth takes the last step towards being Boaz's wife. To achieve that, she adds yet another factor in the third clause. She says to Boaz, 'You are a redeemer'. Unlike Naomi, she does not speak of 'our' redeemer. He is 'a' redeemer, but strictly speaking, according to the law, he does not have any clan obligations to her, a foreigner. By the way in which she expresses herself throughout v.9b, with 'I' as the first word and 'you' as the last, she shows what the issue is: 'I' and 'you'. 'Things must be resolved between you and me, directly and immediately, without any reference to YHWH's wings,' is what Ruth is in fact saying to Boaz. She cannot force him. The choice is his and it is a free one, though the fact that he is a redeemer can give him a moral obligation. But he has to choose, for or against someone who is a stranger in this land.

In the early morning

After Boaz's reply, Ruth continues to lie in the place at his feet (3.14). When she gets up, it is still dark and impossible to discern one man from another. That is also a good thing, otherwise another man could recognize her as a woman on the threshing floor. She gets six measures of barley from Boaz, but according to the text she does not say any more to him.

In the early morning Ruth gets back to her mother-in-law. We do not know whether it was dangerous to go through fields and along paths in the dark. Nothing is said about this. She tells her mother-in-law everything that Boaz has done for her (3.16b). But who can tell what that was, whether anything happened, whether they lay in one another's arms or only talked; whether they enjoyed making love? As readers, we have heard nothing of this. The narrator, apparently deliberately, simply says succinctly, 'And she told her all that the man had done for her.' 'All' could mean anything.

Then Ruth says something that we readers have not heard before. She tells Naomi that Boaz has given her six measures of barley with the words, 'You must not go back empty-handed to your mother-in-law' (3.17). It is not clear whether Boaz really said this or whether Ruth is acting as if Boaz has said it. As readers we know that she gets barley, but we know nothing of the explanation that Ruth gives of this. Ruth also proved to have given her own interpretation of Boaz's words in the previous chapter. Boaz is said to have told her that she had to go with the young men, whereas what he had actually said was that she had to stay with the young women. For the second time Ruth suggests to Naomi remarks of Boaz which certainly were not indicated by the narrator's account. As readers, we cannot be certain whether we are getting Ruth's view here or that of Boaz. But we have an indication. Ruth is the only one who could have heard Naomi remark on her arrival in Jerusalem, 'I went away full and I have returned empty' (1.21). Boaz had not been present. At that time Naomi was not referring so much to her empty stomach (for on the way out there was a famine and on her return home there was not), but to her empty belly or womb. She felt empty because she no longer had any offspring.

Ruth now uses this same word 'empty'. Here she is making it look as if Boaz is suggesting that these fruits which fill the stomach contain the promise of other fruits, namely fruits which will fill the womb. Thus Naomi is presented with hope of something more: according to Ruth, as a hopeful sign the grain points forward to future descendants.

In Ruth's own words

I was well content with the life that I was leading in Bethlehem. I was living with Naomi, and for the time being we had enough to eat. Later I would see how things went. But Naomi had changed. She was no longer the pitiful person she had been in Moab and during the first weeks in Bethlehem. She saw a new future dawning and had devised a dangerous plan. It was certainly ingenious, but devising plans is easier than carrying them out. I wasn't immediately keen on trying it. What a risk I would run! Boaz is such a great lord, and I would have to . . . I let her convince me, but not whole-heartedly.

And there I went. Well washed and smelling of fragrant oil, I went through the fields to the threshing floor. The sun had already gone down. The stars were in the sky. The moon was full and went along with me. Slowly I began to become reconciled to the whole enterprise. Naomi was right. She said what I had so often said to her in the past: there is no way without going, there is no goal unless you set it yourself; and there is no meaning to your life other than the significance that you give it. I thought about all this as I went along, but also felt that recently I had lost this feeling. I had been so busy gleaning and getting a small supply of food for the summer that I was happy just sitting at home. But unless you keep going you'll never arrive. This time Naomi had to make it clear to me what I must do. So you see that you can learn from one another, and two-way traffic is possible even on a road which does not exist. To begin with I was afraid that I would have to tow Naomi along all my life. Who could have thought that one day she would set me on the way?

And there I was, going through the fields on tiptoe. With the moon and God at my side I was content. 'There is no way except to go on the way,' I hummed to myself. We shall see what comes of it. There was lots of noise coming from the places whether the men had been threshing. They had cleaned the tools, washed with the water that was left in the jars and had begun to eat and drink. I watched everything from behind an olive tree. I was no longer afraid, just fascinated. Normally a woman never goes to the threshing floor in the evening or at night. It was a pretty sight. I crept a bit closer and watched from behind a bush. The wine began to take its effect and the talking and laughing got louder. I could have sung without their noticing me, but of course I didn't.

Boaz was the boss. You could see that clearly. Everyone treated him with respect. Even when they had drunk a bit too much, they still continued to be courteous to him. As far as I could see, he didn't drink a lot. But he did enjoy his food. It was a long time before the meal and the talking were over. I began to get rather cold, though it was a nice spring night and I had put a coat on. I was glad when everyone went to sleep and Boaz, who was last, went to lie down by the heap that had been threshed. In the morning the wagons would come to take the owners' produce to their own barns. It was a big harvest this year and the yield was very large. I've always been bad at estimating, but at a guess I would think that there were a couple of hundred baskets of grain, and they still hadn't finished threshing. Moreover the piles of grain took up a good deal of the threshing floor. A man lay sleeping by each pile of grain; usually it was the owner, but sometimes also one of his servants; without a guard a thief could quickly get away with part of the harvest during the night. Boaz lay resting by a great pile of grain in the furthest corner of the threshing floor, which was veiled in deep darkness. It was difficult to make him out, but fortunately I can see well in the dark. Very carefully, step by step, I tiptoed there. I was terribly frightened when someone began to cough somewhere, but after that it remained quiet.

Suddenly I was standing at Boaz's feet. It was so dark that I had almost trodden on him. Quietly I took my upper garment off. Then my undergarment. It was very strange. I felt the wind on my skin. I went to lie down on my clothes so that I didn't feel the cold coming up from the ground. I lay there comfortably. Boaz hadn't noticed anything; he sighed gently in his sleep. Otherwise it was deafeningly still. The heaven seemed like a great tent spread over the threshing floor. I didn't feel afraid, it all seemed so normal. I don't know precisely how long I lay there like that. I think that I even dozed off a bit. It will have been around midnight when Boaz woke up startled. He turned over and noticed that someone was lying at his feet. He immediately saw that it was a woman, but he didn't know who. He whispered, 'Who are you?' I had my answer ready. I'd had plenty of time to think about it.

After that all went well. After the event I could say that I'd expected that it would, but that isn't true, since beforehand I'd been uneasy about it. The risk that I had to take was also so great. Just waiting to see how things went. I had nothing more planned, except that there was no point in brooding. It's better to go home and tell Naomi everything.

Through Boaz's eyes

Boaz, a man with properties

Naomi has spoken and Ruth is on her way to the threshing floor, where Boaz is enjoying his supper cheerfully (3.7). After that, he goes to sleep at the foot of his pile of grain. Ruth comes and lies down quietly and then the text goes on:

3.8a   Around midnight it happened
        that the man woke up startled,
        turned over
3.8b   and behold there was a woman lying at the place by his feet.

This is a unique verse in the book of Ruth. It is the only time that we look right through someone's eyes: 'behold there was a woman lying at the place by his feet.' The perspective is that of Boaz. By putting it this way the narrator quite explicitly asks us to look with Boaz, for the reader already knows that Ruth has gone to lie down there. Here we see what he sees. We feel what he feels and experience the fright he gets. A woman is lying there. At the same we discover that Boaz here is not called Boaz but 'the man'. And what he sees lying there is not Ruth but 'a woman'. He could think that he was still dreaming, and there-fore cautiously asks, 'Who are you?' Perhaps the dream is con-tinuing; perhaps he's hallucinating. But no, the woman raises herself a little and begins to speak.

There are a man and a woman lying on the threshing floor. At that time a threshing floor had the same associations for readers as a seashore in the setting sun has for present-day filmgoers. All the conventional pre-programmed lights begin to flash. On this threshing floor we look through the eyes of the man. First all is dark. Gradually the contours become visible: something is lying there. No, not something but someone. It's a naked women. But he does not see that she is Ruth, since he knows her only clothed and veiled. In an earlier part we already saw this man and this woman together, but then the stage was dominated by young men and young women. The woman on the threshing floor was one of these young women. There was a gulf, a difference in age and status between the older man and the younger woman. Now things have changed.

The woman begins to speak. 'I am Ruth your maidservant, you are a redeemer.' And what does he do? He reacts in a mood of joy:

3.10a 'Blessed are you by YHWH, my daughter,
     for with this goodness you have surpassed the former;
10b You have not gone after the young men
     whether poor or rich.
11a Now, my daughter, do not be afraid.
     All that you have said,
     I will do for you.
11b For all the people at the gate know
     that you are a strong woman.'

Boaz praises Ruth because she has not gone after the young men, but after him, an old man. And he says, 'All that you have said, I will do for you. For all the people at the gate know that you are a strong woman.' Finally it becomes clear why the narrator in 2.1 used such a comprehensive formula to describe Boaz as 'a man, a hero, strong'. The word 'man' was totally superfluous in this formula. But the moment that Boaz calls Ruth 'a strong woman', the reader knows that this man and woman make a good couple. Moreover it is characteristic of both persons that they express their deepest heartsearchings through remarks in the mouths of others. Ruth did that to Naomi through words of Boaz. Boaz now uses the people in the gate as spokesmen. According to Boaz, these people know that Ruth is a personality. And so he indicates what he feels: 'We are made for each other, two persons, both strong and active people.'

But even two strong people are dependent on the approval of others. So everything must be completely according to the rules. The whole gate may then know that Ruth is a strong woman; no one may know that this woman has been on the threshing floor (3.14). The one piece of knowledge is not the other, as already emerged when Naomi said to Ruth that she must not make herself known to the man on the threshing floor, but that Ruth must choose the right place. A good supply of knowledge is of basic importance. Being a personality therefore does not just mean having strength, power or money, but also knowing how to measure out this power. Energy and patience need to be applied at the right time and in the right way. In this sense Ruth and Boaz are equally matched. They are both people with properties; they know how to combine action and waiting. Power does not just mean grabbing, imposing, conquering, but also manoeuvring. They are both good at manoeuvring: the one acting more, the other waiting more, with everything depending on the rules of the game.

Ambiguity on the threshing floor

Now does Boaz only talk on the threshing floor or does he do anything? Nowhere does it say 'he lay with her', far less 'he went into her', though both are already lying on the threshing floor. Anyone who has often seen films in which first two people are lying in bed, then the picture gets darker, and then a breakfast scene follows, is well aware of what has happened in the meantime. Just as a viewer needs only half a picture, so the reader needs only half a word. Moreover the readers conclude that 'it' was done on the threshing floor, without the text needing to devote many words to it.

But was it? As a reader one could well imagine that Ruth was already 'married' to Boaz at the end of Chapter 3, but is that being rather premature? Chapter 4 would be superfluous if the marriage were already consummated in Chapter 3. In that case the scene in the gate would even be shamefully misleading. The question there is who shall marry Ruth, the other redeemer or Boaz. This discussion is out of place if, shortly beforehand, Boaz had had sexual contact with Ruth. Moreover 4.13, 'Boaz took Ruth and she became his wife and he went into her', would be completely out of order. It is not out of modesty that the narrator does not say anything about what went on on the threshing floor. Given the way the story continues, it is impossible to presuppose that Boaz and Ruth had sexual intercourse on the threshing floor. From the point of view of the text that is ruled out. Probably the problem lies in the reader's head. The reader is the one who jumps to conclusions on the basis of general expectations. The ambiguity is in his or her head, not in the text.

Or is it? What are we to think of the vocabulary in this scene on the threshing floor: the word 'come' that can also mean 'go into'; 'know' that can also mean 'have intercourse'; 'lie' that can also mean 'lie with'; the word 'feet' that can also denote 'the sexual parts'; and the word 'uncover', which is clear enough? These terms are all ambivalent. None of the words is in itself sufficient to allow the conclusion that the meanings are meant to be sexual, but the accumulation of this kind of word certainly has this effect on the reader. The selection of these terms by the narrator, all of which have a sexual undertone, seems deliberate. The clash between the story line which excludes sex on the threshing floor and the words with a sexual overtone causes the ambiguity in the text. This ambiguity is not just in the mind of the reader, but also in the text itself.

It is clear from many biblical stories how narrators tell a story: they describe the actions that the characters perform and make these characters say a great deal. So we alternate between looking with the narrator and looking with a (main) character in the text. Emotions, musings or unconscious levels are seldom described in biblical narratives. Thus we do not read here in the book of Ruth that 'on the threshing floor Ruth certainly felt afraid, but also found herself attracted to Boaz', far less that 'she felt that she was lying there against her will, but continued to do so because she felt that it was the only solution'. This is the way in which present-day writers enable readers to experience and feel what is going on in someone's head. In the stories of the Hebrew Bible characters hardly ever indicate their motives. They do not display their emotions explicitly; they don't weigh things up carefully; they don't ask themselves whether what they are doing is right or whether they shouldn't take a quite different approach; they have no unconscious bonds with their mother, their father or Oedipus. That doesn't mean that these people didn't have these feelings or thoughts; just that the texts don't show them. But a narrator wants to show the emotions that the characters have. Here in the scene on the threshing floor he does so by creating a tension between the clear line of the narrative and the ambiguous lines of meaning. The ambiguous meanings of the words clash with the story and at the same time produce friction.

In the actions related in this story, sexual intercourse between Boaz and Ruth does not occur. The dénouement has to wait until the following chapter. At the same time the vocabulary of the scene indicates that the atmosphere was erotic, and that there could have been sexual contact. The words thus indicate what is detectable below the surface. The ambiguity allows us to feel what the characters experienced. The narrator leans heavily on the ambiguity of the language in order to build up the emotional tension, the erotic atmosphere, without breaking off the story line. Therefore not only Ruth and Boaz feel this tension, but also the reader.

Boaz's promise

In all this tension, perhaps as a result of it, Boaz speaks at length. At the beginning and the end of his speech he invokes YHWH:

3.10a Blessed are you by YHWH, my daughter,
     for with this goodness you have surpassed the former;
13a If he is not willing to redeem you,
     I will redeem you,
     as truly as YHWH lives.

Surprised by Ruth's audacity, Boaz begins to praise her goodness and calls down YHWH's blessing on her. But in contrast to the first time, when he speaks with Ruth in the field, he no longer leaves it entirely to YHWH to react. He sees that a task has been laid on him, and he also promises to make a contribution: he will be her redeemer. And he endorses this promise with an oath to YHWH. These two references to YHWH, the blessing and the oath, form the framework within which Boaz's long reaction stands (3.10–13).

Boaz has keen perception. In the field he is the first to recognize where Ruth's goodness lay. At that time he described it as 'everything that you did for your mother-in-law (*ch.mot.ch*) after the death (*mot*) of your husband, that you left your father, your mother and the land of your birth, and have come to a people that you did not know before' (2.11). He is positive about Ruth because she has both left what was familiar and has attached herself to Naomi. Here on the threshing floor he is again the person who accurately evaluates what Ruth's second, even better, deed consists of. He says that she despised her own contemporaries in order to find a redeemer in an old clan relation and that she is ready to marry this old man, this redeemer. He recognizes that she is combining the fact that he may possibly be a redeemer with a marriage to him, so that both the name of Naomi's dead husband and the name of Ruth's dead husband can live on. He senses that the dead are an important reason for Ruth's action. Inspired by her, Boaz also makes a connection between redemption and marriage, and calls her appeal to him an impressive act which surpasses even her previous good deeds.

In short, Boaz praises as Ruth's first good deed the fact that by opting for Naomi she stands up for her living mother-in-law (*ch.mot.ch*) without abandoning the dead (*mot*). Ruth's second good deed is that by opting for Boaz, she gives priority to the dead (*mot*) without abandoning her mother-in-law (*ch.mot.ch*). It emerges from Boaz's words that he understands that her dead husband is important for her. It is therefore difficult to decide who or what weighs more heavily for Ruth. Evidently for Ruth her mother-in-law and her dead husband are indissolubly bound together. Through the dead she stands up for the living, and through the living she stands up for the dead.

It is often others who assess someone at their true worth. That applies not only to Ruth, whom Boaz regards very positively, but also to Boaz himself. In 2.20 Naomi says of Boaz:

2.20a   Blessed is he by YHWH
for his kindness has not forsaken the living and the dead.

Of course this is very like what Boaz says about Ruth:

3.10a   Blessed are you by YHWH, my daughter,
for with this goodness you have surpassed the former.

Boaz and Ruth are like each other not only in strength but, in the view of others, also in goodness. They are therefore a suitable couple for restoring the clan bonds which were broken by the deaths of Elimelek and Mahlon.

The use of the term *chesed*, here translated 'goodness', is eloquent in this connection. Ruth does good deeds by going with Naomi and being prepared to marry Boaz, although strictly speaking she is not obliged to. Boaz's good deeds are that he allows Ruth to glean between the sheaves and even has extra ears dropped for her, and that he is prepared to be a redeemer for Ruth and Naomi, although strictly speaking he is not obliged to. It is this combination of freedom and responsibility that characterizes his *chesed*. It is a form of loyalty, of trusting in someone and, on the basis of that trust, taking a risk. Moreover whenever this word *chesed* appears in the book of Ruth, it is explicitly connected with YHWH. Naomi's wish for her daughters-in-law and Boaz, and Boaz's wish for Ruth, is that YHWH will reward them with goodness. But because *chesed* presupposes free will, it also means that YHWH is completely free to give this goodness. He, too, is not obliged to do so.

An open end on the threshing floor

Boaz promises to redeem Ruth, but the picture changes the moment it proves that there is someone who has more right to redeem her. Thus, Ruth may not marry Boaz but another man, as yet unknown. Then all her energetic efforts will have been in vain. At first Naomi seemed not to be able to get any help from her kinsfolk. Finally Boaz was found to be a helpful relative, and now there proves to be a second suitable relative. That's far too much of a good thing.

There is not only another, closer, relative, with clan obligations; Boaz also says that he will let this other man have the first opportunity. This other man may redeem her if he wants to. Boaz will act only if this other doesn't want to. However, before anything happens, Boaz again proves to be a kind man. He says that Ruth must go to sleep. At dawn he urges her not to tell anyone that she has been on the threshing floor. If that were to become known, the whole plan for the redemption would fail. So here Boaz is already creating some conditions for the redemption procedure to go off well. Moreover he says, entirely of his own accord, that Ruth must take off her shawl and get up. Then he weighs up six measures of barley and pours it into the shawl. It is not clear whether by this he wants to give a hopeful signal to Naomi, as Ruth herself will later tell Naomi. Certainly his readiness to do something is evident, but everything no longer depends just on him, and that is what makes the story so exciting. No one knows how it will turn out.

In Boaz's own words

There she lies, so vulnerable. 'Everything valuable is vulnerable.' Who said that? Lucebert, I believe, but it doesn't matter. It expresses precisely what I feel. In everyday life I come up against much harshness. Everyone tries to become richer, to earn even more money, to be even greater, better-off or stronger. Above all people who can be ruthless in their search for power. I live among these people, I meet them, and I'm often one of them. In the gate where rulers and people in authority are active, in the market where traders and farmers have their say, at home discussing with other business people, only one thing counts: being too clever for the other. I'm used to it: hardness makes me harder, thoroughness makes me more thorough, and cleverness makes me cleverer. But I've never come across someone who is so vulnerable. She confronts me with herself in all her nakedness. And by that I don't mean just the physical attraction that she exerts. That someone dares to offer herself in that way, without any masks, without verbal violence, without status and without being backed up by anyone else, has moved me deeply.

It's not that I'm a good person; the word chesed *doesn't suit me. I'm simply dumbfounded that anyone can act like that in these times. For as everyone knows, these are hard times in which we live. Many people are hungry, few have power and food. It's a hard fight. But here's someone who fights not with hardness but with weakness. She's an alien, someone who doesn't have any recognized position in our society. Perhaps it's precisely because she's an alien that she can hold up a mirror to us. That's what a person looks like without a place in society, with no political or social power, no money. She's not afraid to lie there naked, waiting. To dare to show one's weakness is for me the greatest sign of strength. It's much easier to let yourself be seen in your strength or be admired in your beauty, power or status. When I looked into her naked face and saw her unclothed body I knew it: 'An incredible power emanates from this woman.' She won my heart. I'm ready to stand up for her, and through her I'm also able to show my vulnerability.*

I'm changed. I too want to show other people my strength by daring to be weak. Unfortunately I know the others. They aren't easy to persuade. I must try to convince them thoughtfully and discreetly. They're not keen on too much vulnerability. I regret that. They keep running round in their own circle of belief in status, money and goods, and sometimes also their God, without ever having this experience of experiencing the naked other in the flesh. I can only tell my story and hope that people will feel it speaks to them. No more. I can try to do my best for her, but I can't ensure that all these aliens after her will be recognized and accepted for what they are. That makes me sad. For most people know only the force of the word of power or the hard hand. They appreciate far too little the power which goes out from the powerless word. They miss a lot.

Ruth 4: Life Goes On

1a   Boaz went up to the city gate
      and sat down there.
      And look, the redeemer passed by
      of whom Boaz had spoken.
      He said,
        'Come over here
        and sit down,
        Mr So and So.'

1b   He came
      and sat down.

2a   He took ten men of the elders of the city
      and said,
        'Sit down here.'

2b   And they sat down.

3a   He said to the redeemer,
        'The plot of land which belongs to our brother Elimelek,

3b   Naomi, who has come back from the land of Moab,
      is offering it for sale.

4a   I, for my part, said,
        "I shall inform you of it and say,
          'Acquire it,
          in the presence of those who are sitting here,
          and the elders of my people.
          If you want to be the redeemer,
          redeem.
          But if you do not want to be the redeemer,
          tell me,
          so that I know.
          For there is no one but you to redeem it,
          and I come after you.'"'

4b   He said,
        'I shall redeem.'

5a   Boaz said,
        'The moment you acquire the land
        from the hand of Naomi,

5b   you are also acquiring Ruth, the Moabitess, the widow of the
         dead man,
       to maintain the name of the dead
       to his inheritance.'

6a   The redeemer said,
        'I am not able to redeem,
        lest I ruin my own inheritance.

6b   You take over my right of redemption
       for I am unable to redeem.'

7a   This was formerly the custom in Israel in redeeming and
        exchanging:
       to confirm a matter
       a man took off his sandal
       and gave it to the other man.

7b   This was the customary attestation in Israel.

8a   The redeemer said to Boaz,
        'Acquire it yourself',

8b   and he took off his sandal.

9a   Boaz said to the elders and all the people,
        'You are witnesses today
         that herewith I acquire
          all that belonged to Elimelek
          and all that belonged to Mahlon and Chilion,

9b   from the hand of Naomi;

10a   that herewith I also acquire Ruth as my wife,
         the Moabitess, the wife of Mahlon,
         in order to maintain the name of the deceased
          in his inheritance,
         so that the name of the dead is not cut off
          from his family and the gate of his city.

10b   You are witnesses today.'

11a   All the people who were at the gate and the elders said,
        'We are witnesses.

11b   May YHWH grant that the woman
       who comes into your house,
       shall be like Rachel and Leah,
       who together built up the house of Israel.
       Be strong in Ephrathah
       and proclaim a name in Bethlehem.

12a   May your house be as the house of Perez
       whom Tamar bore to Judah,

12b   by the seed

that YHWH may give you through this young woman.'

13a   Boaz took Ruth
and she became his wife
and he went into her.

13b   YHWH gave her conception
and she bore a son.

14a   The women said to Naomi,
'Blessed be YHWH
who today has not left you without a redeemer.
May his name be proclaimed over Israel.

15a   He shall be for you a restorer of life and fullness for your old
age.

15b   For your daughter-in-law who loves you bore him,
she who is better for you than seven sons.'

16   Naomi took the child,
set him on her breast
and became his foster mother.

17   The neighbouring women proclaimed him a name
saying,
'A son is born to Naomi.'

17b   They proclaimed his name Obed.
He is the father of Jesse, the father of David.

18a   These are the descendants of Perez.

18b   Perez was the father of Hezron,

19a   Hezron was the father of Ram,

19b   Ram was the father of Amminadab,

20a   Amminadab was the father of Nahshon,

20b   Nahshon was the father of Salmah,

21a   Salmah was the father of Boaz,

21b   Boaz was the father of Obed,

22a   Obed was the father of Jesse,

22b   Jesse was the father of David.

Through Boaz's eyes

At the gate

The intimacy of the threshing floor is over. From now on everything takes place in the public arena *par excellence*, the city
gate. For a walled city, this forms the point of contact with the
outside world. Such a city gate usually consisted of two gates,
one in the wall and the other around twenty yards inside it. The

space between these outer and inner gates was walled, forming a kind of square. Often some rooms were built against the side walls of this square which were used for discussions during legal cases or in negotiations.

The city gate was the heart of a city. Almost everyone had to pass through the gate twice a day: the men morning and evening to and from their fields, the women in the evening to and from the spring or well. People would be going in and out the whole day. Anyone who wanted to meet someone else, to have a quiet chat, or to know what was going on in the city, had to go to the gate. Not only was there a small square in the gate, but behind the gate on the city side was a much larger square, and this was the social, legal and economic centre of the city. This was where the city authorities exercised their power. They could retreat to the smaller square within the gate for confidential discussion and reflection; in the square outside the gate anyone could present his case for the consideration of the elders and everyone present; the discussions could be heard and the promises endorsed.

From this square, along the inside of the city wall ran a circular street with large houses on either side, the so-called four-roomed houses. These consisted of three rooms with an inner court; sometimes they also had a room on the the first floor. The rich people lived in these houses. Small alleyways ran deeper into the city, giving access to a maze of houses. There was no community oversight of buildings and dwelling so everyone built his own little house without supervision. This usually consisted of one room, sometimes with a little area beside it; cooking was done outside in the street. Because everything was on top of everything else here, there were always conflicts: over the cooking, over the right to free passage, or over the ovens. All these things were presented to the elders in or by the city gate.

In the book of Ruth, Bethlehem is presented as a (small) city with a city gate and thus with a city wall. Behind it ran a circular street along which were larger houses, and with alleyways along which the many small houses were packed together. In this place you could imagine that Boaz had a four-room dwelling and Naomi a tiny single-storey house. Boaz is one of the powerful men in the city, and as one of the elders is often involved in legal cases. An elder (the term literally means one who has a beard) is not a very old man, but can be any man with a beard who is the head of a family. Such a head of a family can play a part in governing the city. At this time 'old' is more or less synonymous with 'wise', and wise does not mean, as it does in the Greek world, a philosopher or someone who reflects a lot on the world, but someone with experience of life or someone who acts well on the basis of knowledge and insight. (Thus a carpenter can be called wise, if on the basis of insight he is a good carpenter.) The elders in the gate are wise by virtue of the fact that they both know the legal rules and have been present at leading cases so that they know jurisprudence. As well as quarrels between neighbours, they deal with the right of aliens to asylum, levirate marriages, problems of virginity on marriage, questions of divorce and squabbles over property.

Boaz is captivating

Boaz goes up to the gate and sits down. He invites ten of the elders of the city to hold a session. Fortunately the very man he has to talk about has just gone by. Boaz had spoken about him earlier to Ruth; he is the one who is closely related to Elimelek. The narrator calls this man 'the redeemer', which is not a proper name but a designation of his function. Boaz addresses the man as 'Mr So and So.' That sounds rather odd. Why doesn't Boaz use the man's name? Surely the clan of Ephrathites can hardly have been so large that he didn't know the name of a fellow member of the clan? Only a few verses later, in 4.6, it becomes clear why neither the narrator nor Boaz gives the man's name. As often in the Book of Ruth, someone's name becomes clear from what he or she does. Thus for example, Naomi, the lovely, shows that she was lovely, but has become bitter. 'Mr So and So' doesn't deserve a name because he is not willing to maintain the name of the deceased. The one who does not allow the dead to have a name is not granted a name himself. He is doomed to remain anonymous.

Boaz addresses this kinsman, since they have to come to an agreement in the presence of the elders who appear as witnesses. Boaz begins immediately with the land of 'our brother Elimelek' and says that Naomi is offering this for sale. So far we have heard nothing about a piece of land. Naomi has not mentioned it, nor has she used the word 'sale'. Is Boaz fantasizing here? Probably not, since as so often in a text things only become clear the moment that someone talks about them. For example, Naomi said that Boaz was a redeemer, whereas up till then we readers had heard nothing about this. We heard it from her mouth. In a similar way, Elimelek's land has always been there.

After first mentioning the land belonging to Elimelek and Naomi, Boaz shifts the perspective to 'Mr So and So' and himself and says,

4.4a   I, for my part, said,
           'I shall inform you of it and say,
              "Acquire it,
              in the presence of those who are sitting here,
              and the elders of my people.
              If you want to be the redeemer,
              redeem.
              But if you do not want to be the redeemer,
              tell me,
              so that I know.
              For there is no one but you to redeem it,
              and I come after you."'

Boaz begins with 'I'. It is no longer a matter of Elimelek or Naomi, but of two kinsmen here on the square by the gate, 'I' and 'you'. Earlier we saw that the moment that characters have a special concern, they begin to speak through the words of another person. A direct form of address is then embedded in a indirect form. That is also the case now, and because Boaz cannot cite anyone else, he puts his direct speech into his own speech and says, 'I, for my part, said, "I shall inform you of it and say, 'Buy it.'"' And as readers we then know that we have to pay attention, because something is about to happen here.

Being forewarned counts double, but what Boaz says seems very simple. He uses the word 'redeem' four times. 'Will you redeem or shall I?' is his question. It seems so simple, but there's a catch. That only becomes clear when 'Mr So and So' reacts and says, 'I shall redeem.' That should have settled the matter, since Elimelek's land would then remain in the clan and the fellow-clansman would look after it in the future. But then Boaz speaks again and immediately points out to the man an implication which has not been mentioned hitherto.

4.5a Boaz said,
          'The day you acquire the land
          from the hand of Naomi,
5b   you are also acquiring Ruth, the Moabitess, the widow of
              the dead man,
          to maintain the name of the dead
          to his inheritance.'

The relative must not only redeem the land but also marry Ruth. There is no rule that marriage and redemption go together, but only a possibility. However, Boaz presents this as a condition: if the relative redeems he has to marry Ruth, The son who is born of this alliance can preserve the family of Elimelek from extinction and link the name of Elimelek permanently with the inheritance. 'Oh no,' reacts the anonymous kinsman, 'I can't do that', and he takes back the word that he has previously given. Now that it emerges that he also has to take Ruth, he says 'No'. Why? Is it because Ruth is a Moabitess, as Boaz does not neglect to mention?

   To understand the key to the negotiation between Boaz and the anonymous friend, let's look again at verses 4 and 5. In verse 4 Boaz indicates what the question is. There is a childless widow, Naomi, who is selling the property of her dead husband, Elimelek. Because her sons are also dead, the property threatens to be lost to the clan. A fellow-clansman who comes forward as redeemer can take upon himself the double task of both taking over the property of the dead kinsman and marrying the widow, so that the child which is born will be able to provide a name for the property. So far there are no problems. The kinsman knows that he can acquire both the land and the widow, and moreover it is no more than logical that he should think that the widow in question is Naomi. And strictly according to the law that is the case. Naomi is the one whom the kinsman must marry in order to keep the property for the clan. But Naomi is already old, and because of her age in all probability she will not be able to have any more children. The relative would therefore have no problems in both marrying her and acquiring Elimelek's land. In the long run his own children would come into possession of Elimelek's land.

Then Boaz immediately names Ruth as the widow. Hitherto the anonymous kinsman has not realized that Ruth is the widow in question. Moreover he could not have realized that, because the mention had been only of Naomi's land. This new information provided by Boaz changes things completely. Ruth is young and will certainly be able to bear a son; and this son will not only inherit Elimelek's heritage, but will also share in 'Mr So and So's' own heritage. The kinsman had not foreseen that, and it is something that he does not intend. Boaz puts him on the spot by arguing as if widow Ruth were in the package to be redeemed, whereas hitherto only widow Naomi has been mentioned. That is Boaz's trick: he exchanges one widow for the other. He couples widow Ruth with the land, Elimelek's heritage, and that is possible because Mahlon, the son of Elimelek and Ruth's husband, is also dead.

Boaz is a man who is strong but at the same time subtle in his actions in the gate. He remains within the limits of the law, but also manoeuvres skilfully. Boaz presents a really captivating argument, which is captivating in both senses of the word. It is captivating and fascinating because through his game of questions and answers Boaz shows up the kinsman's real concern: profit, and not the continuation of the name of the dead. Boaz unmasks the relative's train of thought. The argument is also captivating because at the same time it holds the anonymous kinsman captive. He has no way out, and therefore has to withdraw. Moreover he says, 'You redeem. I shall not, I can't, I don't want to. Please take over my right as redeemer.' The anonymous potential redeemer proves not to want to be a redeemer and quickly withdraws. He leaves the restoration of the clan property and the preservation of the names to a member of the clan who is less closely related.

Immediately after that the matter is settled. Mr So and So takes off his sandal in the presence of the elders and all the people, and with the sandal hands over the right of redemption to Boaz. While doing this he says, 'Acquire it yourself'. And that settles the matter. Through this gesture and these words the agreement becomes valid.

Stratego

The book is very like a game of Stratego. Three eminent strategists are competing on the field of life. Ruth is the first and most original of them. She opts to leave Moab and become an 'alien' in order to follow her mother-in-law Naomi to her people. However, gradually she proves to have not only opted for her mother-in-law, but also for her dead husband. She is bold in her request to glean in the field behind the reapers, but she is both heroic and tactical at the same time above all in her visit to the threshing floor. Following Naomi's plan she undresses herself on the threshing floor and lies naked at Boaz's feet. Through her request to Boaz, 'Spread your cloak over me', she shows that she is a master at the strategic game. She presents Boaz inexorably with a choice. And he opts for her and promises to exert himself in the gate. Her plan has worked. Unfortunately, there is also another kinsman who has the first right to redemption. If Boaz can get rid of him and Boaz 'marries' Ruth, she will have completely succeeded in her plan to secure both the future existence of her mother-in-law and the future name of her dead husband.

Under Ruth's influence, Naomi, too, has gradually become more enterprising. At first weary of life, she gives herself over to melancholy and bitterness. But stimulated by Ruth's activities, she begins to become more hopeful. As a native woman of Judah and a believer in YHWH she allows her faith to be corrected by this foreigner. Thus Naomi undergoes a radical change. Under Ruth's influence she no longer leaves everything to YHWH, but herself devises a war plan that must bring Ruth into close contact with Boaz, a distant relative of her husband. Her scenario for the threshing floor is daring, even if Naomi limits the risk as far as possible by arranging the time and place of the encounter precisely. However, there is no avoiding Ruth's actual task: 'Take off your clothes and go and wait in the place at his feet.' On her own initiative, Ruth is to add a cunning request, but Naomi is the one in charge, and she has devised the broad outlines of the strategy. The risk that Ruth runs is great. If things go wrong, Naomi will also suffer, for how will she get by as an older widow? However, Naomi's plan succeeds brilliantly.

Finally there is Boaz, a man who from the beginning is presented as an enterprising and strong person, although he does not get round to doing anything for Naomi on her return or for her daughter-in-law on his own initiative. He is probably well aware that he is a possible redeemer, but because someone else is more closely related, he does not need to take on anything. Nevertheless Boaz is ready to allow Ruth to glean ears of grain on his field after the reapers, and he deliberately asks his servants to leave ears behind for her. He is a good man, but in the first instance it is not his business to support Naomi and Ruth in a structural way. Naomi's and Ruth's plans are intended to make him change his mind. Through Ruth's initiative on the threshing floor he is prepared to go much further than before. He devises a plan, and in so doing gives an indication of his great strategical insight. Precisely because as an elder or head of a family he is well aware of how the legal regulations work, he is in a position both to remain within the law and to get what he wants through two tricks. His first piece of cunning is the 'exchange trick': he keeps widow Naomi for the acquisition of the land and exchanges her for widow Ruth in order to produce descendants. The second trick is that he lumps the dead men together. By speaking of 'the name of the dead' in the plural he can make the names of both Elimelek and Mahlon live on in the heritage. Thus brought under the same heading, all their names can be preserved. Naomi had already said something in 2.20 which is gradually becoming clearer: 'Boaz's goodness doesn't abandon the living and the dead.' Just as 'Mr So and So' doesn't deserve a name because he doesn't grant others a name, so Boaz fully deserves his name because he grants others a name and doesn't abandon either the living Naomi and Ruth or the dead Elimelek, Mahlon and Chilion; *bo'az* really doesn't do *'azab*.

Boaz and Ruth

In his last words, Boaz is now addressing the elders in the gate. We can infer from the formal and precise wording that this is the standard formula for concluding a process of redemption.

4.9a   Boaz said to the elders and all the people,
  'You are witnesses today
   that herewith I acquire
    all that belonged to Elimelek
    and all that belonged to Mahlon and Chilion,
9b   from the hand of Naomi;
10a   that herewith I also acquire Ruth as my wife,
    the Moabitess, the wife of Mahlon,
   in order to maintain the name of the deceased
    in his inheritance,
   so that the name of the dead is not cut off
    from his family and the gate of his city.
10b You are witnesses today.'

The indentations in the translation show how well Boaz's argument is constructed. The framework is provided by the elders, who are witnesses to the agreement between Boaz and the anonymous kinsman. This involves Boaz in buying both the property of Elimelek, Mahlon and Chilion, and Ruth as a wife, with the aim of keeping the name of the dead in existence. The elders in the gate can regard Boaz's words as the formal confirmation of the transaction and so bear witness to their agreement in the future if need be.

But more is involved here than a standard procedure of redemption. Right at the heart of his argument Boaz shows that his concern is Ruth, whom he mentions in v.10a with both her name and her surname. In both v.9a and v.9b he has already prepared the transition to her. For in now interpreting to the elders what he had previously described to 'Mr So and So' as the property of Elimelek as being both 'all that belonged to Elimelek' and 'all that belonged to Mahlon and Chilion', he is not making the extent of the property greater; rather, with the introduction of Mahlon he is also including Ruth. Immediately afterwards, he mentions Ruth's name and identifies her as both a Moabitess and as wife of Mahlon. Thus in an original way Boaz smuggles Ruth into the redemption procedure. Ruth is a foreigner, someone who really cannot be redeemed, yet in a redemption procedure Boaz buys both the property of the dead from Naomi and the hand of Ruth. This redemption or restoration of the clan is thus quite different from others. Boaz makes the name of the dead men of Judah live on through a foreigner! The fact that the elders in the gate nevertheless do not oppose the redemption is due to the fact that Boaz presents everything as normal and as falling within the standard procedure.

And so the marriage of Boaz and Ruth takes place. We have been able to share in all the phases in the development of the relationship; we have felt the tension, weighed up the opportunities and now it is settled.

4.13a   Boaz took Ruth
        and she became his wife
        and he went into her.
13b   YHWH gave her conception
        and she bore a son.

Simplified: that's the least that one could say. Here is the long-prepared-for report of Boaz's first sexual contact with Ruth. The foreplay on the threshing floor lasted longer than the climax. Moreover the emphasis is not on the sexual climax, far less on the nine months of pregnancy, which are dismissed in four words. Everything turns on the son who is born. Mother Ruth does not appear in the story again. With this delivery she has made her last contribution to the book.

Formerly Ruth had been married ten years to Mahlon without becoming pregnant. The text now gives the impression that she becomes pregnant immediately. The cause of this is not just Boaz, though he makes an unmistakable contribution, but above all YHWH, for the child is not just the product of human sexuality but at the same time a gift of YHWH. This is the only time in the whole book when the narrator writes that YHWH acts directly. Earlier in 2.12 Boaz had expressed the wish to Ruth that YHWH would reward her and complete her work. But at the moment when she has become 'full' in 4.13, otherwise than

Boaz expected, he is the one who has made the contribution. At the same time his activity alone is not sufficient, since YHWH has 'given' both the conception and the pregnancy. And so it becomes clear that YHWH is not active solely and without mediation, but always with human co-operation. It is the same with Ruth in Chapter 2. Ruth then exerted herself in order to survive, but at the same time she knew that everything did not just depend on her; she called what she hoped for 'grace'. She acted and waited: on the fields, on the threshing floor and in Naomi's house while Boaz was at the city gate. She was not waiting for Godot, but her patience was a hopeful waiting for the growth of what she herself had sown earlier. Dedication and strategic action do not give either Ruth or Boaz the vain idea that anything is possible. On the contrary, both are characterized by a combination of going and gift. Ruth's surrender, Boaz's going in and YHWH's gift are here attractively summed up in one verse.

In addition to grace, for the first time Ruth also finds rest. At the beginning of the book Naomi's wish for her daughters-in-law had been that they should find rest in the house of a husband, a rest that YHWH would 'give' them. Orpah then returned to find rest in her own land. Whether she did so, we readers do not know. Ruth did not go in search of rest. She undertook a whole series of activities which brought unrest and insecurity, and at the end of the book she gets a child who offers rest and security both to her dead husband and to Naomi. Thus the new-born son fulfils Naomi's need and creates a name for the dead man. He links the survival of the mother-in-law (*ch.mot.h*) with the survival of the dead husbands (*mot*). Thus Ruth, the one who did not seek rest, has given rest and security to others, and in so doing has also herself found rest. We hear no more of Orpah, and of the other person who wanted rest and security, the anonymous kinsman. These two, 'Mr So and So' and Orpah, resemble each other, in so far as both dissociate themselves from an enterprise which involves much effort and uncertainty, and opt for what is normally called 'the sensible way'. They are less concerned with 'giving' than with 'getting', and the result is that they get hardly anything extra. By contrast, in this book those who choose the uncertain way, or make a

way for themselves, like Ruth, Naomi and Boaz, finally get the
surplus of the gift, or grace.

In Boaz's own words

*I don't know what's come over me. I'm an old man. Life hasn't
treated me badly. I've a respectable house, devoted servants, a
good place in the city gate. I will certainly have made some
mistakes, but I don't remember them any more. I've always
made an effort and respected the legal regulations. And as a
result I myself am respected. I'm called a strong man, and I am,
but even strength has its limits. The shadow side of this strength
is that you think that you're doing it all yourself, that everything
depends on you and your insights. The shadow side of power is
that you no longer look through the eyes of a child but with the
eyes of a ruler. Everything is ordered by your look, everything
planned by your order, everything thought of in terms of your
own views, even God. For God usually serves to support or
legitimate your own insights. With God at your side you have
the world in your hands. It's so strange, and I'm now realizing
more and more clearly that under and despite all that respect
and reputation, and even with all that right on my side, I've
always been lonely.*

*Of course I was in love once, indeed more than once. Some-
times I even had a woman, but that didn't make my solitude any
less. It was as if she made the strings of melancholy vibrate even
more loudly in me. I had my work, and also my conversations
with the others in the gate. And above all after a disturbed
night, it's good to find rest in the status that others accord you.
The lullaby of power, of knowing what is going on, of plans and
strategies, sounds sweet in your ears. The pleasure of the power
game is so great, and in the gates of other cities that pleasure is
just as great; sometimes this power even become so important
that cities go to war with one another. That certainly happens if
in such a city men have the say who think that their group
represents the only true kind of man. Above all a strong leader
can ruin a people, the kind of leader who impresses on his
people that the others are different, so different that they're
hardly even human, to make it easier to slaughter them like*

*animals. It may be Gilead or Moab, Sarajevo or Vukovar,
Baghdad or Mogadishu: the others are always presented as
being the kind that deserve to be beaten and trampled on. 'May
Almighty God help us,' people are fond of saying. And they go
to battle, always with God on their side. Indeed there must be
heavenly hosts to be able to fight in all these wars.*

*Right is easy, since it's always on our side and never on the
side of these alien guests who enter the land. The right of one's
'own' property, of the ancestors who have lived on the same
land and have their own language-group and culture. It has
been a grace to find someone like Ruth. She showed me the right
of the other, and by her courageous behaviour she showed me
how to look through her eyes. I still well remember the first time
that I saw her in the fields. She struck one as foreign. Our
language has an attractive word for 'foreign': 'someone who
catches your eye'. I saw her, but didn't see with her eyes. The
darkness on the threshing floor made me see. The gate gave me
the words, and I've become another person. No longer so sure
of my rights, of the insights of my eyes. Now that I've come to
look at things differently, I'm no longer in a position to put my
old eyes back in my head. It's just like looking at a rainbow.
Once you've seen the colours of light, you've experienced something that was always there but that you've never noticed. Ruth
is my rainbow, or perhaps I should say that together we are a
rainbow: together we give colour to our existence and make
tangible what was always present in us.*

*Ruth has shown me how boundless her love is for Naomi,
for her dead husband and for God. We people of Judah, and
above all we people of Bethlehem, think that God is bound to
frontiers. I also used to think that myself. 'Our God is the God
of all creation, but his believers stop at the frontiers.' That was
my conviction. Now that I've come to look through Ruth's eyes,
I've discovered how short-sighted I've been. As if our God is
dependent on human frontiers! God isn't made in the image of
us human beings, though many people think so. We are made in
God's image. His image transcends us and takes us over our
frontiers. Moreover Ruth has shown me just how unbounded
her love is. Even the boundaries of age have not kept her from
loving me. And that's special. For plenty of (younger) people*

don't call themselves cosmopolitan when it comes to territorial frontiers, but are very rigid when they have to look beyond the frontiers of their own age-group. Ruth is different. In fact she's much younger than I am, but that doesn't seem to disturb her. Through her, the song of loneliness has fallen silent for ever in me. She has given me both this boundless feeling and a son, who will make me and others live on beyond the boundaries of death. My son, my wife, my love.

Through the eyes of the men at the gate

The standard blessing

The men who witness Boaz's testimony react in chorus with a marriage blessing. Like the other women, Ruth is not present at the gate, and thus she perceives nothing of this wish for happiness, though it will also be meant for her. Evidently it is enough for a marriage blessing to be pronounced man to man:

4.11a   All the people who were at the gate and the elders said,
       'We are witnesses.
11b   May YHWH grant that the woman
       who comes into your house,
       shall be like Rachel and Leah,
       who together built up the house of Israel.
       Be strong in Ephrathah
       and proclaim a name in Bethlehem.
12a   May your house be as the house of Perez
       whom Tamar bore to Judah,
12b   by the seed
       that YHWH may give you through this young woman.'

In the first instance, as a reader one is inclined to think that the men in the gate are composing this wish on the spot. If one thinks this, it's strange that they speak of Ruth as a young woman. The word *na'ara* which is used is used throughout the Hebrew Bible only for an unmarried woman, and it's a long time since Ruth was that. It's also surprising that they also wish for a widow who was barren for ten years and was left childless a family as large as the twelve children of Israel. Finally, it is also incomprehensible that these elders should spontaneously devise such a well-structured text. It is far more probable that this text is not a blessing which they have composed specifically for Boaz and Ruth, but a standard wish that they often pronounce at 'betrothals' or 'marriage ceremonies'.

This kind of fixed blessing contains stereotyped remarks about fertility derived from life in Judah. In this milieu, Rachel and Leah are the ancestral mothers of the twelve tribes of Israel, and Tamar is the matriarch of the Ephrathites, the most important clan in Bethlehem. The wish for girls or young women who are going to 'marry' is that they should bear many children for Israel and Bethlehem, just like the three ancestral mothers. It is then striking that the men in the gate also use this standard formula for Ruth, since Ruth does not come from Bethlehem, is not a woman of Judah, and is not even a young girl. It is also remarkable that they use this blessing for Boaz, who is no longer a young man, but a man of ripe age. Probably the men in the gate are used to reacting formally in a situation like this. They feel that they have some support if everything is being done correctly and in accordance with the rules of the game.

The undercurrent

When the men in the gate express their conventional wish for blessing and mention the names of Judah and Tamar, we are reading more than they know. The elders know nothing of what happened on the threshing floor, but we readers do. They are unaware of the similarity between what happened there and what took place between Judah and Tamar. Nor are they aware that Ruth resembles Tamar, above all in that both indicate his duties of redemption to the man they have in view by taking off or putting on clothes. By their behaviour they try to make the name of their dead husband live on. Boaz and Judah resemble each other in age. Both are old men who through union with a young woman restore a broken clan bond. However, one difference is that Tamar had rights and Judah obligations, whereas Ruth, as a foreign woman, has no rights, and Boaz, as a redeemer in the second degree, has no direct obligations. They are in a certain sense 'volunteers'.

In their standard prayer the elders also mention Rachel and Leah. Moreover, it is striking that Rachel is a very apt comparison with Ruth. Rachel remained barren for a long time and only became pregnant when YHWH opened her womb, whereas after a ten-year marriage Ruth was childless and remained so up to that moment. The wish that Ruth 'may be as Rachel' opens up for her the perspective that YHWH will open her womb and that they will have children. Thus however much the comparison with both Tamar and with Rachel serves as a stereotype for other women, it is very appropriate for Ruth. The word 'strong' that the elders use in their exhortation 'be strong in Ephrathah' is equally very suited to these two people. In a standard prayer this clause would have only a general sense, in the sense of 'show strength and prosperity'. Here, however, it has taken on a specific undertone, since Boaz was described earlier as 'a strong man' and Ruth as a 'strong woman'. Together they can form 'a strong pair'.

Perhaps this strength applies even more specifically to Boaz and Ruth. In order to see that, we must pay some attention to the tripartite structure of the blessing. The first wish, that Ruth may have as many descendants as Rachel and Leah, is separated from the third wish, that Boaz may get as many descendants as Perez, by a second wish: 'be strong in Ephrathah'. Literally, *chayil* means physical or psychological strength, and physical strength also includes sexual potency and the capacity for procreation. The wish of the leaders, some of whom know what it means to be getting old, is that Boaz, who is also no longer in the prime of youth, shall be virile and potent enough to give Ruth a child. That also explains, from the perspective of the speakers, the reference to Judah and Tamar. Like Boaz, Judah was an old man who despite his age had twins by Tamar; a clearer sign of Judah's potency was hardly possible. In short, all three parts of the blessing spoken by the men in the gate refer to procreation. Even the appeal to YHWH to make a contribution to the fertility of this couple shows the specific function of what normally is just a vague and general wish. For this time YHWH's support is a bitter necessity for the older Boaz and the barren Ruth.

The conclusion should be clear: this blessing uttered by the men in the gate is meant as a standard formulation, but in the present text it functions as a blessing which is tailored to this unique situation. Only the reader and Boaz can perceive and evaluate these two levels, since the elders do not have the same information. Thus the book of Ruth gains depth through the fruitful clash between the general and the specific, and between the text and the reader, who recognizes and evaluates the confrontation between the overtone and the undercurrent in the text.

Through the eyes of the women

Naming names

The men have spoken in the gate and other men have listened. Because male voices are regarded as normative, this settles the legal matters. Thereupon Boaz takes Ruth as his wife and the text speaks immediately of conception and birth. Only then do the women speak. They have no legislative or judicial power, but they have a considerable capacity to assess things. They pronounce their evaluation and pass their judgment, but of course they do not do this in the open space of the gate, which is no place for them, but indoors. Like the men, they speak only to members of their own sex, and in so doing they address Naomi. We might ask what she has to do with it. Surely it's Ruth who has given birth? However, the significance of this will gradually emerge.

Some months previously the women had asked just one question on Naomi's return to Bethlehem: 'Is that Naomi?', and Naomi had given a lengthy answer. Now it seems as if they are returning to the answer which Naomi had given them then.

1.19b   They said,
          'Is that Naomi?'
20a   She said to them,
          'Do not call me Naomi (Lovely),
20b   call me Mara (Bitter),
          for the Almighty has made me very bitter.
21a   I went away full,
          and YHWH has made me return empty.

21b   Why do you call me Naomi,
            YHWH has borne witness against me,
            the Almighty has done me evil.'

4.14a   The women said to Naomi,
            'Blessed be YHWH
            who today has not left you without a redeemer.
            May his name be proclaimed over Israel.
15a   He shall be for you a restorer of life and fullness for your
                old age.
15b   For your daughter-in-law who loves you bore him,
            she who is better for you than seven sons.'
17a   The neighbouring women proclaimed him a name
            saying,
            'A son is born to Naomi.'
17b   They proclaimed his name Obed.

On Naomi's arrival in Bethlehem the women needed only to ask
Naomi a simple question to make her burst out in a tirade full
of accusations against God. At the end of the book the women
again address Naomi, but this time Naomi says nothing in
reply. The women easily fill in the space that has been opened
up.

    In both texts, three times we have the expression 'proclaim a
name' (*qara shem*). In the first conversation between the women
and Naomi, Naomi kept talking. 'Don't call me Naomi', 'call
me Mara', 'why do you call me Naomi?' Since at this time the
name was regarded as an indication of a person's nature, with
the change of name, Naomi is referring to the change in herself.
In returning to it here, the women are giving a final evaluation
of Naomi. First of all they show that Naomi has received a
different answer from YHWH from the one that she herself indicated. Naomi used the Hebrew word *'anah*, which means both
'answer' and 'bear witness against', in the second meaning of
'bear witness against', in order to describe YHWH's behaviour
towards her. The women now demonstrate that Naomi has
indeed received an answer from YHWH in the person of Obed.
The answer which YHWH gives indirectly to Naomi is not
witness against her, but a son for her. The name that the women
give to the child is 'Obed', which means 'he who serves (YHWH)'.

Here at the same time the women are indicating what Naomi's response to YHWH's answer could be: instead of accusing YHWH she needs to serve YHWH just like her (grand)son.

The women also give Naomi back her name in another way. Naomi had evocatively said, 'I went away full, YHWH has made me return empty.' The women of Bethlehem now say to her:

4.15a   He shall be for you a restorer of life and fullness for your old age.

Naomi was empty and has now literally been filled again. She has gone all the way from full to empty, and from empty to full. According to the women, from today she can again feel that she is Naomi, the lovely, for her (grand)son gives her strength of life (*nephesh*). This *nephesh* is the principle of life that God blows into the human being's nostrils in Genesis 2.8, which makes this a living being. It is this vital strength which now returns in Naomi. She who seemed more dead than alive is again full of life; her life has been filled, and her days have become worth the trouble of living. So the women celebrate the return of Naomi. As far as they are concerned there can be no misunderstanding: everything turns on Naomi. On Ruth's arrival in Bethlehem they take no notice of her; on the birth of Ruth's son they speak only to and about Naomi. According to them, the book of Ruth is more about Naomi and her homecoming than about this foreign woman. Perhaps if the women had had their say, the book would have been called 'Naomi' rather than 'Ruth'.

Ruth, the full daughter

But the women of Bethlehem appreciate Ruth more than we first thought, for after what they say about her son they add:

4.15b   (. . . and fullness for your old age.)
        For your daughter-in-law who loves you bore him,
        she who is better for you than seven sons.

It is a long time since Ruth has been called 'daughter-in-law', *kalotah* (written without vowels as *klt*). In 1.6 and 1.7 Ruth and

Orpah are described as Naomi's daughters-in-law, and in 2.20 and 2.22 we read that 'Naomi speaks to her daughter-in-law'; after that the term 'daughter-in-law' does not appear again. In 4.15 characters in the story use this word for the first time. It is the women of Bethlehem who give this name to Ruth; at the same time they add an extra connotation by putting it next to the word 'fill', *kalkel* (without vowels *klkl*). In this way they make it evident that the terms 'daughter-in-law' and 'fill' both contain the root *kl*, 'full': the daughter-in-law (*klt*) bears a son who fills Naomi (*klkl*). Perhaps instead of daughter-in-law it would be better to speak of full-daughter: as a daughter Ruth ensures that Naomi is filled.

The women are reacting to Naomi's reproach that YHWH 'made her return empty' (1.21). The women of Bethlehem deliberately use the same (causative) form, 'make to return', which does not appear elsewhere in the book of Ruth, in speaking of the new-born son. According to Naomi, YHWH is the cause of her returning empty, and according to the women, Ruth's son is the cause of the return of Naomi's life-force. By bearing her son, Ruth sees to it that Naomi returns from a situation which is characterized by emptiness, not-living and dying to full life.

Whereas throughout the book all the attention is directed towards a son, and everyone looks towards this son, it is very striking that the moment the son is born, the women conclude that daughter Ruth is worth much more than a son. She is even worth more than the ideal number, the 'fullness' of seven sons. This daughter and her love for Naomi distinguish her from other daughters and sons. And so at the end of the book Naomi and the readers are convinced by the women of Bethlehem that however important a son may be, this daughter Ruth is even more important. The book has rightly been given the name of Ruth.

Mothers

The narrator takes over from the women. In three short sentences he describes what Naomi does and then for the last time allows the women of Bethlehem to speak again:

4.16   Naomi took the child,
          set him on her breast
          and became his foster mother.

17   The neighbouring women proclaimed him a name
          saying,
              'A son is born to Naomi.'

How revealing this verse is! In every respect it seems as if not Ruth, but Naomi, is the mother of the child. First of all Naomi 'takes' the child, whereas shortly beforehand in 4.13 it was stated that 'Boaz took Ruth'. Perhaps this means that Naomi just takes the child, but it is also possible that she takes over the child from Ruth. The term 'take' is the best rendering of this ambiguity in the Hebrew, because it can mean both take up and adopt. In the second clause Naomi sets him on her breast. In Hebrew the phrase can mean both 'she put him to her breast' and 'she pressed him to her bosom'. The third clause says that Naomi becomes 'his foster mother'. The word *omenet* which is used here can mean both foster mother and wet nurse (the latter meaning occurs, for example, in II Samuel 4.4). Just as on the threshing floor, it looks as if the narrator is deliberately using words which are ambiguous. Naomi can either be a foster mother, which is biologically the case and fits the story line precisely because Ruth has given birth to the child, or a wet nurse, which is biologically impossible and in contradiction to 4.13, but fits the statement that she feeds him or gives him her breast. This latter interpretation is confirmed by the explanation of the neighbouring women, 'a child is born to Naomi' (4.17). Here it is clearly stated that the child is Naomi's. Ruth has disappeared from the stage; now Naomi is said to be the mother. It is her child that is born, not Ruth's. And so the story is rounded off: at the beginning of the book, Naomi had lost her 'children' (1.5); now Naomi has a child back again.

The threads which together form the fabric of Chapter 4 form a multicoloured pattern. In the gate, in conversation with 'Mr So and So', Boaz lumps together the two widows. By making the transition from widow Naomi to widow Ruth, Boaz was in a position to connect Ruth with both the land and with a marriage. He did all this in the presence and with the agreement of the men in the gate. Now the women also lump the two mothers together. By making the transition from mother Ruth to mother Naomi, they are in a position to begin to see Naomi as mother of the child. They are both mothers of the same child; they are both heirs to the same land. Both the men and women and the narrator make mother-in-law and daughter-in-law one widow and one mother. Those who at the beginning of the book of Ruth were so different because they differed in starting point, nationality, age and faith, gradually grow towards each other. Inspired by Naomi, Ruth is converted; inspired by Ruth, Naomi changes in her belief and behaviour. Ruth and Naomi are one, and at the same time different.

Fathers in place of mothers

With that the role of the women is played out. We do not hear the neighbouring women again, and Ruth and Naomi disappear into the wings. The men take over once more.

17b	(Obed . . .) He is the father of Jesse, the father of David.
18a	These are the descendants of Perez.
18b	Perez was the father of Hezron,
19a	Hezron was the father of Ram,
19b	Ram was the father of Amminadab,
20a	Amminadab was the father of Nahshon,
20b	Nahshon was the father of Salmah,
21a	Salmah was the father of Boaz,
21b	Boaz was the father of Obed,
22a	Obed was the father of Jesse,
22b	Jesse was the father of David.

The book begins with a man of Judah who goes to Moab and dies. His two sons die and the camera shifts to the surviving widows Naomi and Ruth. With no children and no future they go on the way to Bethlehem and keep their heads above water. Gradually they become visible, and their byway becomes the highway of the book. But now, right at the end of the book (4.17b–22), these women are again put on a byway. The he-way is again the high way: everything now turns on Obed, the father of Jesse and David. The genealogy which follows is impressive:

ten generations culminate in the procreation of David, the great king of Israel. Boaz, the father of Obed, stands in seventh place in this genealogy. Ruth, the wife who is worth more than seven sons, marries the man in seventh place, the place of fullness, in the line leading to David. And so Boaz proves to be the hero of the book, and not Naomi or Ruth. Or perhaps Boaz is not the hero but David, since the book of Ruth ends with his name.

It is a realistic end. It bears witness to a sense of reality, since that is how things now go on. Women can undertake all this, but history is written in the name of men. One could even say that the whole book of Ruth is a prologue to this genealogy which has got out of hand. After all, it is the genealogy of King David: that, and not a sentimental story about two women, is the highway of history. Of course, these are clever women, but the ordinary course of events goes on. And this is controlled by men. Isn't it?

Possibly, however, the undercurrent of the book undermines this realism and this pattern which generally applies. It is a specific feature of this book that under the normal course of events a line runs in which a foreign woman and an indigenous women survive against the stream and fill their lives in an original way. Such a genealogy doesn't change anything here; at most it can form an appendix or epilogue to the book. Otherwise the story of these two women probably wouldn't be included in the Bible. All right, the concession has now been made and the men and the king David followers can now be reassured, and that is important, for they form the basis of history (= his-story). But the women of Bethlehem have already summed things up in their convincing conclusion: Ruth is worth more than seven sons. Seven is the figure of fullness or completion, and thus more than ten. So Ruth is also worth more than a genealogy of ten sons. The title of this book proves the women of Bethlehem right: the book is not called Boaz, Obed or David, but Ruth.

Ruth 1–4: Through the Eyes of the Narrator

The narrator in historical perspective

Historical dating of the book of Ruth

Knowing the time in which a text was written makes some difference to reading and understanding it. A text fulfils a particular function, depending on the time in which it was composed and the public for which it was written, and thus is told differently. Compare, for example, one of Chaucer's *Canterbury Tales* written in the fourteenth century with a modern novel. The biblical book of Ruth was similarly written at a particular time with a view to a particular audience of listeners and readers. We, men and women of today, read the book, but of course the author did not have us in mind when he told his story. By whom was it written? Was it a man, or possibly a woman? For whom is it told, and what was the function of the book? What did the author intend with his story? If we are to be able to discover that, we need to know something about the time in which the book of Ruth was written.

There are two divergent views of the time in which the book of Ruth was written. The first is that the book was written in the time of King Solomon, around the tenth century before the beginning of our era. The second is that it was written after the Babylonian exile, in the time of Ezra, i.e. five centuries later. Just imagine that the book that you are holding in your hand at this moment could be by Julian of Norwich or Ellen van Wolde! In the case of English books, we can tell from the language that they were written at different times. The problem with an ancient language like classical Hebrew is that so little is known of the development of this language. It is certain that from the seventh century on, imperial Aramaic, the language of the Assyrian and Babylonian empire, exercised increasing influence on Hebrew. Traces of this are visible in the Hebrew texts of the Bible, and we call these Aramaisms. Sometimes words are taken over from Aramaic; at other times it is a matter of endings or grammatical forms. This influence is comparable with the influence of English on Dutch in the second half of the twentieth century. Something of the same thing also happened between Aramaic and Hebrew. In the last two centuries before the beginning of the Christian era Hebrew was totally penetrated by Aramaic.

In the case of an ancient text like the book of Ruth it is difficult to arrive at a reliable dating on the basis of language alone. It is in fact possible that Ruth was not composed all at once by an author, but that different 'hands' or redactors were involved in it in successive periods. Thus Ruth could first have been told orally as a family history, later written down, and revised yet later for a contemporary public. It is also possible that 1.1–4.17 was written at one time but that in another period a genealogy, now 4.18–22, was added. Moreover Aramaic influences on the Hebrew of Ruth can indicate a late date of (part of) the book or a later revision of the text. Archaic Hebrew phrases or words are evidence of either an early date or a late date; in the latter case the use of archaic words will indicate a desire to give the impression that this was an ancient text. In short, language alone is insufficient as a criterion for the dating of a text.

Legal customs are perhaps a more reliable criterion for dating a book like Ruth. The book of Deuteronomy describes many legal customs, especially in chapters 21–25. Now as legal customs and statements occur in the book of Ruth which also appear in Deuteronomy, we know that the book of Ruth was written after Deuteronomy. And since it is generally assumed that the book of Deuteronomy was written in the seventh century BCE, Ruth would be after that date. Such legal customs do in fact appear in Ruth: the process of redemption, levirate marriage, the custom of handing over a sandal in a transaction, and the spreading of a cloak over a woman as a sign of a proposal of marriage. One might think that here we finally have a firm criterion for the dating of Ruth. Unfortunately that is not the case, since these legal matters appear in Ruth in an unusual way. Normally speaking, redemption or buying up a clan possession (see Leviticus 25) takes place separately from a levirate marriage (see Deuteronomy 25), whereas in the book of Ruth these are connected. Another difference is that in the case of a levirate marriage Deuteronomy speaks only of a brother-in-law, i.e. a brother of the dead man, and not of another relative in the clan, as in Ruth. Perhaps indeed we have to say that strictly according to the letter of the law (Deut.25.5–10), in Ruth there is no question of a levirate marriage, since there is no *levir* or brother-in-law, but only a distant relative. Another great difference between Deuteronomy and Ruth is that the law book is about obligations, whereas in Ruth there is no question of an obligation but only of a voluntary choice.

Two opposed conclusions can be drawn for the dating from these legal matters. On the one hand one could say that the laws which are formulated in the book of Deuteronomy were not so precisely defined and formalized at the time of Ruth. This argues for an early dating of Ruth. On the other hand, one could say that the laws of Deuteronomy were already so old that they began to be used in a distinctive way and combined. This would point to a late date for Ruth. Finally, one could also conclude that the occurrence of legal rules and customs in a literary narrative like Ruth cannot give any indication of the dating of the book. A characteristic of a literary text is that by means of language it creates a 'world within the text'. Here much from outside the text is worked over in an independent way and so the world of the text does not agree with existing historical reality.

There is therefore only one other possible criterion for dating this book of the Bible, namely a comparison with other texts in the Hebrew Bible. In style and narrative structure, the book of Ruth seems very like the patriarchal narratives in Genesis. Moreover, in its 'both feet on the ground style' it is like the stories about David and Solomon in the books of Samuel and Kings. This should argue for an early dating of the book of Ruth. On the other hand, the theological content strongly resembles that of the book of Esther. In both Esther and in Ruth we have women who win a 'victory'. Because Esther is a late book, this would argue for a late dating. Finally, those who support this late dating argue, the book of Ruth is deliberately given a nostalgically archaic atmosphere to make it resemble the patriarchal narratives in Genesis. A similarity to a famous ancient text like that about Abraham serves to emphasize the worth of the new (= late) book. In short, even comparisons with other biblical texts do not allow us to draw any definitive conclusions about the date of the book of Ruth.

As is quite clear, dating a book of the Bible is a matter for specialists, who can argue for a long time over the interpretation of small details. In going on to put the book of Ruth in its time and giving a description through the eyes of the narrator, I am working on the basis of the arguments I have cited. Here narrator 1 is the one who narrates the book of Ruth in the time of Solomon. Looking through his eyes we see that he has quite a different aim from narrator 2, who lives in the time of Ezra and envisages other readers.

Through the eyes of narrator 1

In the centuries before David and Solomon were kings, the land of Canaan consisted of many rival cities, the armies of which were regularly fighting one another. David was the first ruler to be in a position to conquer a larger number of cities and districts in the south (Judah) and the north of Canaan, which he brought together as one kingdom, Israel. He became king over this kingdom and made Jebus, a small city which he had conquered from the Jebusites, its capital, changing the name Jebus to 'Jerusalem'. From there he began to govern his kingdom, which for the most part consisted of Canaanites, with a small minority of YHWH believers. The Canaanites were the indigenous inhabitants of the land and had a fertility religion with Baal the bull god and Astarte the goddess of grain as their most important deities. By contrast, the YHWH believers were not indigenous, since their distant ancestors came from Mesopotamia (present-day Iraq) and Egypt. They differed from the others in their belief that YHWH was the only God. The indigenous population and the YHWH believers lived side by side in David's new kingdom, and each made sacrifices to their gods in their own way and on their own altars.

David's son and successor Solomon extended the kingdom. He strengthened the structure of government, built a temple and a palace, and made the city of Jerusalem a fairly large centre of government, trade and religion. The trade, agriculture and international commerce increased greatly, as did the burden of taxation. More and more people of Canaanite origin converted to belief in YHWH, since it had become clear to them that this God was more powerful than Baal. Many of the foreigners who came to live in Israel similarly adopted belief in YHWH. In addition, a large part of the Canaanite population continued to worship their own gods. Thus under Solomon the population was a great mixture of Baal believers, foreigners who had not converted, and YHWH believers.

The book of Ruth could have been written at this time. The main indications in the text for this early dating are as follows. First of all, the language of Ruth is early Hebrew and is very like that of Genesis, Samuel and Kings; the similarity between Ruth and the patriarchal narratives in Genesis is particularly great. Moreover the Hebrew of Ruth is quite different from the late Hebrew of Esther, Chronicles or Nehemiah. Some examples of archaic linguistic features which occur in Ruth are the form used for 'I', the lack of any differentiation between grammatically male and female forms, and the frequent lack of the so-called *matres lectionis*, i.e. letters guiding a correct pronunciation. Furthermore the laws or precepts which are described in Ruth are far from being as formalized as they are in the later book of Deuteronomy. This also becomes evident in the openness towards Moab which is characteristic of the book of Ruth. There does not seem to be any hostile atmosphere between Judah and Moab, whereas in Deuteronomy dealings with Moab and marriage with a Moabite woman are strictly forbidden. Furthermore, how could David be described as someone who was descended from a Moabite in a time when the legislation of Deuteronomy was normative? No, the book of Ruth must clearly date from long before Deuteronomy.

During Solomon's reign, scribes were appointed to set down the great deeds of kings David and Solomon in writing, and this resulted in (parts or redactions of) the books of Samuel and Kings. Later, people began to describe what the period before the monarchy was like; there is an account of it in texts which later came to be called the books of Judges and Joshua. The stories about Abraham, Isaac and Jacob, which hitherto had been handed down orally, were possibly also written down in this period. The book of Ruth could also have been written at this time as an answer to the question how foreigners were to be treated in the time of Solomon, with all those outsiders, whether Canaanites or foreigners, who wanted to convert to belief in YHWH.

The story of Ruth takes place in an area then known to everyone, namely in Bethlehem in Judah, the place which had been made famous by its great son David. Through the narrator this story shows how it was possible for David himself to be the descendant of a Moabite woman. The reason lay in the conversion of this woman. She came to believe in YHWH and stood out for her good behaviour. So she becomes a worthy ancestor of David, since her faith in YHWH made her part of the tribe of Judah. That can also happen to others who do not believe in YHWH: by having faith like that of Ruth, they can form part of YHWH's people. Thus the book of Ruth is to be described as a book 'aimed at compromise'. The narrator tells his story from the perspective of those who believe in YHWH, and to support the view that it must be possible to accept foreigners into one's own people. Everyone should know that faith in YHWH is the only thing that counts. Just as Ruth the Moabite opted for YHWH and his people, so any foreigner can opt to become part of Israel.

The narrator of the book of Ruth even goes a step further, since he shows that those who believe in YHWH can learn from such a convert. Through Ruth, he can show that belief in YHWH is both a form of going on the way and a trust in other people and in God, and in this way the book indirectly criticizes those in Israel who hate their next-door neighbours and foreigners, and think that YHWH supports this discrimination. The narrator makes a plea for an belief in YHWH without frontiers and calls on those who believe in YHWH to be open to other people. Are they not themselves foreigners in origin? Certainly the message of the narrator will have sounded unacceptable to the powerful among his hearers and readers. For them it was easier to treat the others as transients and to regard themselves as permanent. They give priority to going back to the rock of their own certainty and identity. Openness to newcomers, who have different clothing, habits and customs, is not so attractive to YHWH believers in the kingdom of Solomon, and often not to others either. Why should they give up what they have? For them the narrator tells the story of Ruth in order to show that YHWH is a God who calls everyone, whether or not they believe in YHWH. This is a summons to foreigners to believe in YHWH, or to others who believe in him to alter their behaviour. Go, go, this YHWH keeps saying. Go yourself, God, most people will have thought. But those who do believe in YHWH sense that they must go and let the others, the foreigners and outsiders, stay. This is a somewhat disconcerting book for those who want to keep the doors closed, who want to remain and demand everything for themselves. That is true not only for the time of Solomon but also for later times. Again and again this book of Ruth could be and can be read as a stimulus to throw open the closed doors of one's own existence.

Through the eyes of narrator 2

The text of Ruth tries to reinforce the impression of being very old by using some dated and archaic words, but that is only a thin veneer. The Aramaisms indicate that the Hebrew has been influenced by the Aramaic which was spoken in the Near East during the time of the Assyrian and Babylonian empires. The legal customs similarly reflect the usages of a later time. Deuteronomy had already been the law for daily life for centuries, and in Ruth there are references to it and developments of it. Moreover, as a literary text the book has taken the opportunity of combining in a distinctive way the matters that are prescribed in Deuteronomy. The practice in Ruth reflects a broader interpretation of the legal obligations in Deuteronomy. The emphasis is not on the obligations but on the fact that a free choice for the rules is better than the obligatory performance of a task. From this perspective, the story of Ruth needs to be seen as a reinforcement of Deuteronomy, since the personal and voluntary choice by Ruth and Boaz to follow the Deuteronomic laws of redemption and marriage emphasizes them more than a compulsory observance of the laws would do.

The historical situation in the period after the exile looks quite different from that in the time of Solomon. No wonder, since five centuries have passed in the meantime. After the heyday of the rule of David and Solomon the kingdom fell apart into two pieces, the northern kingdom named Israel and the southern kingdom named Judah. The fate of people in Israel and Judah was more or less random, depending on which kings were ruling and the international political situation. In the eighth century BCE the Assyrians captured the northern kingdom and carried off a large part of the population into exile in Assyria. In the sixth century the Babylonians took over rule from the Assyrians and occupied Judah. They deported the elite, the leaders of the government, priests, scribes, the rich and the merchants, from Judah to Babylon. The top people in politics, the economy and religion from other conquered territories were also deported to Babylon. The Babylonian tactic was to make the population defenceless by transporting the know-how from all regions to Babylon. They were particularly succcessful in doing this. In Babylon the different groups lived in separate districts (ghettoes) and continued their lives there. The peasants and ordinary citizens in Judah, and also in the occupied regions of Syria, Phoenicia, Asia Minor and Turkey, were left behind. In Judah some of these were Israelites or YHWH believers, and some were Canaanites or believers in Baal.

In Babylon, the people of Judah who had been carried off into exile underwent a process of changing awareness. They suffered a serious crisis of faith and asked themselves how YHWH could have abandoned them. How was it possible that YHWH could have allowed his elect people even to be deported? Gradually, as a result of this crisis, they developed a different picture of God. For example, their God YHWH did not seem to be so bound to a place as they had always thought, and therefore they could serve YHWH without a temple and daily sacrifices. They began to sense that not only the temple cult was important: what counted above all was daily life and behaviour. Here their faith had to become visible. Consequently they began to order the whole of their life by the insights of their faith: the day was ordered by regulations about food and purity; the week by the sabbath; the year by the festivals; and life as a whole by circumcision at birth, solidarity with the weak within one's own group in everyday life, and the rules for burial on death. A whole network of forms of behaviour thus ensured that the people of Judah allowed the whole of their (social) life to be supported by their belief in YHWH. In this way they distinguished themselves markedly from the other groups in Babylon, who began to call them the 'Jews'. They stood out by not working every seventh day, whereas the others did not know such a division, and by maintaining some special regulations about food. It is clear that in Babylon the Jews definitively began to mark themselves off from others as a special group.

When after fifty years the Babylonian empire collapsed and the Persians came to power, the Persians allowed the exiled elites of the peoples, including the Jews, to return whence they had come. First a small group of Jews went to Jerusalem to see how things were and to make preparations for the larger group which would return later. This small group discovered that the population which in the meantime had continued to live in Judah had occupied their houses and had become accustomed to doing without the elite. Those who had remained at home had developed in their own way and their children had married in Canaan, sometimes with YHWH believers and sometimes with Canaanite men or women. They had almost forgotten those people in Babylon, whereas the latter regarded themselves as the true believers. When the people from Babylon returned, there were squabbles over the ownership of houses and land, and also over belief and morality. It will have been rather like the reunion of East and West Germany in our time. After the fall of the Berlin Wall and the official formation of one state, West Germans demanded back the houses in East Germany which they had had to leave fifty years earlier. However, over the years these houses had been lived in by a new generation of East Germans, who all thought that they were their own houses. Furthermore, in the meantime East Germany had undergone a different cultural development, which could not be swept away in a couple of years. If we see how many economic and social problems this reunification brought, we can perhaps feel the tension that was experienced in Jerusalem at that time. New groups kept returning from Babylon and there were constant disputes. There was no cohesion in society and a new structure had to be formed.

Ezra, a leading Jew from Babylon, received a charge from the Persians to take in hand the government and the (religious) reorganization of Judah. The Persians were more concerned to have well-governed territories than chaotic small groups which quarrelled with one another. They wanted the central government of Persia to be respected and as much tax as possible to be paid, and for that they needed as much peace and order as possible to prevail in the empire. In their view it made more sense to restore their own religion and relative autonomy to all the population groups than to impose one religion on all. Ezra made a powerful impact. He felt that the group which had returned had to have the say in the formulation and content of belief in YHWH. Religion and government in both Judah and Israel had to be regulated in accordance with its insights, which had been reformulated in Babylon. Moreover Ezra put a strong emphasis on the sound development of the population and he established extensive marriage legislation (see the book of Ezra 9–10). None of the descendants of former generations which had contracted 'mixed', i.e. Canaanite–Israelite, marriages, were true Jews. Only the YHWH believer who could claim a good, unmixed descent and observed the laws of the sabbath, the food laws, circumcision and the laws of solidarity was a Jew. This solved all kinds of problems: those who had contracted mixed marriages had no right to houses, and for the first time belief in YHWH was firmly attached to ethnic descent. From this moment on a Jew was someone who believes in YHWH and belongs to the Jewish people. Outsiders were neither tolerated nor admitted.

If the book of Ruth was written in this period, we must read it as a protest against the mentality which prevailed at the time of Ezra. The narrator wants to show that this ethnic restriction imposed by Ezra and his followers is unjust, because even King David was partly of Moabite descent. Through the story of Ruth the narrator shows that the choice for YHWH must be the criterion by which foreigners are measured: if they believe in

YHWH and behave in accordance with the spirit of the prescriptions of the law, they can be part of the Jewish people. How can people like Ezra defend closing the frontiers to others, when David, whose worth they can hardly deny, also had a Moabite ancestor? According to Ezra's rules, David should be excluded. Such an inward-looking ethnic legislation is absurd.

Furthermore, were not Abraham and Sarah foreigners who converted to belief in YHWH? Did not Rachel and Leah, both of whom are mentioned in Ruth, come from Mesopotamia, and did not they too become ancestral mothers of Israel? What would Ezra do about that? No, the narrator wants to make clear by his story of Ruth to anyone who will listen that faith and good behaviour are the only things that count. So according to the narrator, membership of Israel need not be limited to ethnic Israelites. Had not the prophets already said before the exile that the important thing was not the formal religion of sacrifices or belonging to the elite group of the rich and the believers, but one's attitude towards the weakest in society? Anyone who, like Ruth, seeks protection under YHWH's wings, forms part of Israel. So those who are Israelites by birth can be inspired in their behaviour by Boaz, the prototype of a good YHWH believer.

The narrator did not choose to write a polemical pamphlet, as that would have been to adopt the same style as Ezra and his followers. With Ruth he has made a book which radiates a kind of inner harmony and power, and he contrasts this rest and equilibrium with the ethnic cleansings and the xenophobia. He is opposed to the rigid criterion which is applied to everyone. In the end, he says, they measure only themselves. He sets the book of Ruth against the closed system of measurement, the certainty of one's own descent and identity. He tells his readers and hearers an attractive story, which carries them along by its style and imagery, and especially by the many possibilities of applying it. From now on people can no longer say, 'We don't know how foreigners see things'; from now on they need to listen to foreigners and look at them, as YHWH himself had listened to them and looked at them when they were themselves foreigners.

Alternative ancestors

The narrator narrates his text with a view to a particular public of readers and listeners, but that audience is not empty-headed. These people themselves have views, convictions and stories going through their heads. By alluding to texts from the tradition the narrator can reinforce the meaning of his own story and give it an extra dimension. Therefore not only has the historical context influenced the meaning of Ruth but also the 'inter-textual' context, i.e. all the other texts which were resonating in the heads of listeners or readers and to which the narrator refers.

Tamar and Ruth

In Ruth 4.12 the narrator makes the men in the gate mention the names of Perez, Tamar and Judah. Prompted by this, the listener or reader compares the story of Judah and Tamar with the book of Ruth. In both stories an Israelite man leaves the place of his birth and his son marries a non-Israelite woman. Sadly, in both cases the son dies childless, and the widow, in the one case called Tamar and in the other Ruth, is left alone. Without a husband and children she finds herself in a hopeless situation. She can only escape from it by attracting the attention of an older member of the family. Ruth succeeds by undressing at night on the threshing floor and Tamar by sitting veiled at the entrance to the city. The result is the same in both cases: the older man of Judah (Boaz or Judah) has sexual intercourse with the young foreign woman (Ruth or Tamar) and she bears a son, who in both cases is referred to as 'seed', what is needed for procreation from the dead husband. Thus both stories give the impression that women are more dedicated than men to the continuation of the Israelite people, whereas they are really outsiders.

But both in Genesis and in Ruth, the Israelite men have good reasons not to feel responsible for the continuation of the family. They are not brothers of the dead husband and therefore they have no obligations under the law. Moreover there is another candidate who comes before them, and they expect him to father a child to the widow. Unfortunately, however, this closer relative who is a candidate in Genesis 38 and Ruth 4 does not feel responsible for the continuation of the family. In Genesis 38.8–9 this is Onan, Judah's second son:

38.8   Then Judah said to Onan,
            'Go in to your brother's wife,
            and perform the duty of a brother-in-law to her,
            and raise up offspring for your brother.'
38.9   But Onan knew that the offspring would not be his;
            so when he went in to his brother's wife
            he spilled the semen on the ground,
            lest he should give offspring to his brother.

This Onan is just like 'Mr So and So' in Ruth 4. Like this anonymous kinsman, Onan does not want to father a child who will continue the name of his dead brother. They both want the pleasures, but not the burdens: Onan is certainly prepared to have sexual intercourse with the widow (often) and 'Mr So and So' to buy Naomi's land, but neither of them wants to do the right thing by the dead man, far less by his widow. All they have in view is their own self-interest, not the interests of any other man or woman.

So there the foreign women sit. One man of Judah does not feel responsible for the continuation of the family because the law puts no obligations on him (Judah or Boaz), while the other (Onan or 'Mr So and So') avoids the obligation. The result is that there are no children. The women have no more possibilities within the law (we can see this in the case of Tamar: if she had been pregnant by another man then she would have been burned by Judah!). They have to take fate into their own hands. And they do this by covering themselves completely or undressing completely. By doing this they disclose both their wishes and their identity. But only in the first instance does this uncovering relate to the women themselves, since on closer inspection it becomes clear that by their behaviour they are above all uncovering the others.

In both texts, Genesis 38 and Ruth, for this we find the key word *nachar*, which means 'see', 'observe', or 'take notice of'. In 2.10 Ruth says to Boaz: 'Why do I find grace in your eyes, that you should take notice of me (*nachar*), when I am "one who is seen", or a foreigner (*nochria*, from the same root *nachar*)?' And later in 2.19b, Naomi says, 'Blessed be he who took notice (*nachar*) of you.' As 'one who is seen', Ruth makes people, including Boaz, see her. In the denouement of the Judah–Tamar story in Genesis 38.25–26, *nachar* plays an even more important role. The moment that Tamar shows Judah his signet, cord and staff, which he has given her as a pledge, 'Judah recognized (*nachar*) them and saw (*nachar*) that Tamar had right on her side'. Thus the word *nachar* forms the nucleus of both stories. As non-Israelite women, Tamar and Ruth are called women who 'are seen', but they are in fact the instruments through whom Boaz and Judah begin to see. Precisely by being outsiders, they hold up a mirror to those within. Although strictly speaking Boaz and Judah have no obligations, Ruth and Tamar indicate that the intention of the law, which is to secure the continuation of the generations, counts more heavily than the letter of the law. Like the men at the centre of government in the gate, Judah and Boaz concentrate all their attention on the obligations and the legal situation according to the rules of the law. If there is a hitch and the legal possibilities are exhausted, the women are the ones who mark out an alternative way in these texts. They succeed in maintaining the people in an inventive way.

The narrator of the book of Ruth pays close attention to Ruth's alternative approach, and various exegetes conjecture from this that the narrator is a woman. In their view, otherwise it is difficult to explain how a narrator can make the readers look so clearly through the eyes of Naomi and Ruth. It would also be difficult to understand otherwise how there is so much attention to the creative contribution of these women to the history of Judah and appreciation of it. By making the men in the gate say that Tamar and Ruth have made the history of Judah possible, the (possibly) female narrator hopes to convince the male readers that these foreign women are indispensable links in the chain of the history of Judah. Without Tamar the people of Judah would not have existed, and without Ruth they would never have got a King David.

Rachel and Leah, Naomi and Ruth

The men in the gate compare Ruth not just with Tamar, but also with Rachel and Leah. Thus they extend Ruth's ancestral function still further. Whereas Tamar is the ancestor of one tribe, namely the tribe of Judah, Rachel and Leah are the ancestors of twelve tribes. The people in the gate refer to them in Ruth 4.11:

4.11   'May YHWH grant that the woman
        who comes into your house
        shall be like Rachel and Leah,
        who together built up the house of Israel.'

Rachel and Leah are the wives of Jacob, who is also called Israel. Leah bears him ten sons and Rachel two, and together these are the twelve tribes of Israel. The men in the gate compare Boaz with Jacob and Ruth with Rachel and Leah. What do we know of these women? Their story is told in Genesis 29–30. Rachel is the attractive women whom Jacob chooses as his wife on their first encounter, but for whom he has to work seven years. Her sister Leah does not attract him, and moreover her name means 'dull' or 'unattractive'. After seven years' hard labour, Jacob gets Rachel as his wife; at least, that is what he thinks, but hardly is the wedding night over than he discovers that he has not slept with Rachel but with Leah. The night must have been very dark for Jacob not to have noticed that the two sisters had been exchanged and that he had got the dull one and not the attractive one. After a week he also gets Rachel as his wife, but for her too he has to work for her father Laban another seven years. During these years Leah has many children, whereas Rachel remains barren. At her wits' end, Rachel says to Jacob, 'Give me children, or I shall die' (Gen. 30.1). Finally Rachel becomes pregnant twice, but a poignant aspect of the story is that she dies giving birth to her second son. Thus it is not her infertility but her fertility which proves the death of her.

What connects Ruth with Rachel and Leah? First, of course the tricks in the night which make Tamar, Ruth and Leah notable women. But in addition there is a more impressive agreement. Just as Rachel and Leah between them have built up the house of Israel, so Ruth and Naomi between them carry on the people. Both pairs of women are also exchanged: Rachel and Leah in the night, and Ruth and Naomi (by Boaz) in the gate. But there is also a difference. 'Between them', Rachel and Leah make their contribution towards building up Israel, but not in a harmonious collaboration. As two quarrelling sisters they produce two series of children, and these children stand for the twelve tribes of Israel. Ruth and Naomi, as one mother, produce the child who more than anyone else will help to build up the unity of the house of Israel.

To some degree, Ruth and Naomi have grown together here. In the first chapter of the book they were still distinct. The change begins in the second part of that chapter with Ruth's unconditional choice of Naomi, after which the two go on the way together. Later they grow even closer together as a result of the events on the field and on the threshing floor. And finally in the last chapter they become one in the words of others, since Boaz lumps the widows together and the women of Bethlehem make the mothers coincide. This is quite different from the story in Genesis about Sarah and Hagar, who quarrel over motherhood and build up two divergent peoples. It is also different from Rachel and Leah, who as jealous sisters together build up the twelve tribes of the people of Israel. Through a harmonious collaboration, Ruth and Naomi are able to become the ancestral mother of the king who will bring together the twelve tribes of Israel under one name. So in this sense, too, the alternative of these ancestral mothers Ruth and Naomi becomes clear: two women, one foreign and one from Judah, are as one woman, the ancestral mother of David. Perhaps it is not such a crazy idea to think that the author and narrator of the book of Ruth is a woman, for here women are not played off against each other, as is usual in the (patriarchal) literature of this time, but work together.

Abraham and Lot, Ruth and Boaz

The relationship between the book of Ruth and the patriarchal narratives in Genesis goes even deeper. This is a matter not just of direct similarities between persons or terms, but of an underlying pattern. One network can be recognized in which both stories can be included and which the narrator offers us in a convincing way.

The book of Ruth as a whole is very like the stories about Abraham and Sarah in Genesis 12–25. In Genesis 12 YHWH chooses a foreigner to become the tribal ancestor of his people and makes him go to Canaan. Moreover we hear of an extra handicap, since Abraham and his wife Sarah are already very old when Sarah finally becomes pregnant. The same is also the case with the book of Ruth. God chooses an outsider to be the ancestral mother of David. This time the woman is not old (through she is childless), but her husband Boaz is old and has remained childless. Being a foreigner and being old characterize both these stories about ancestors. That becomes even clearer if we take account of Naomi as an ancestral mother, for in that case again an aged couple is the basis for the history of Israel.

Abraham goes to a foreign land the moment that YHWH says, 'Go, go' (*lech lecha*', Gen. 12.1). Similarly, Ruth opts for YHWH by going to a strange land (Ruth 1.17). She goes with Naomi and says, 'Where you go, I shall go' (*telchi 'elech*). Both resolve to live in a new land and opt for a new God, YHWH. In the first instance there might seem to be a difference, in that Abraham is chosen, whereas Ruth herself chooses. However, at the end of the book of Ruth it proves that Ruth, too, is chosen by YHWH, to bear a son who will be the forefather of David. In both situations, however, we hear of 'going abroad', of going from the familiar to the unknown. This characterizes both Ruth and Abraham. Here belief in YHWH is indissolubly bound up with going on the way. That this involves great uncertainty emerges from the sequel to the two stories. Abraham gets the promise of land, blessing and descendants; Ruth does not get a single promise. The first piece of the promised land of which Abraham gains possession is the place where Sarah is buried. Ruth similarly gets a piece of land after the death of her father-in-law and husband.

To begin with, YHWH only partly fulfils his promise to Abraham of blessing or prosperity, since without children this promise is not complete. Therefore both in Genesis and Ruth the great point of uncertainty remains childlessness. The doom of barrenness hangs over all. What use is a land and prosperity if you can't hand it on to anyone? Isaac has yet to be born. Certainly at the moment when he departs from the land of his birth, Abraham has the son of his dead brother, his nephew Lot, with him. In the clan and family association he can regard this nephew as his son. Thus despite all his concern, Abraham has some reassurance, because in any case he can live on through Lot. However, unfortunately there is a break-up between Lot and Abraham. This far-reaching event is described in Genesis 13. There the narrator uses the word *parad*, cut or separate, three times, to indicate this. The emphasis on this 'separation' is evident, and 13.11 expresses this poignantly: how is it possible for one man to cut himself off from his next of kin? Lot settles in a neighbouring region, and from that moment on Abraham can no longer live on in him.

Furthermore Lot's fortunes are described separately from those of Abraham, and he does considerably less well than Abraham. The city in which he lives, Sodom, is destroyed, and he loses his wife in the landscape, where she remains behind as a pillar of salt. Only he and his two daughters survive the disaster of Sodom. They retreat into a cave, far from the inhabited world. The daughters have no husband and father Lot is old. The women are therefore afraid that the family will die out. To avoid that they plan a trick (Gen.19.30–38). They make their father drunk, go to lie with him in turns, and have sexual intercourse with him without his noting it. The result of this nocturnal escapade is that they become pregnant. The older daughter of Lot gives birth to Moab and the younger to Ammon. Thus at a great age Lot has become father of Moab and Ammon.

At first sight there seems to be little similarity between the experiences of Lot and those of Ruth. Of course the story of Lot and his daughters is like those of Judah and Tamar and Boaz and Ruth. In all three texts the continuation of the family is in danger and the older figure, whether Lot, Judah or Boaz, is unaware of his responsibility for the family. Happily there are women there who get the seed out of the old(er) man by a trick. And although the stratagems in the night differ (making the man drunk, covering oneself with a veil or taking one's clothes off), the fertilization takes place and the men become the fathers of sons.

However, on closer inspection it proves that the narrator of Ruth makes a connection between the patriarchal narratives in Genesis and his own story which gives the book of Ruth a totally new dimension. The narrator brings out this line at the beginning and the end of the book of Ruth. At the beginning, the narrator puts into Ruth's mouth the key words of the book:

1.16b   'Where you go
         I shall go.
         Where you spend the night,
         I shall spend the night.
         Your people is my people,
         your God is my God.
17a   Where you die
         I shall die,
         and there shall I be buried.
17b   Thus may YHWH do to me
         and thus may he continue to do.
         Nothing but death will separate me from you.'

Ruth says that she will always stay with Naomi, since 'Nothing but death will separate me from you.' The word 'separate' used here, one which does not occur much in the rest of the Hebrew Bible, is the same word *parad* as appeared in Genesis 13. 9, 11, 14. Here the narrator of Ruth brings out the contrast between Lot's behaviour and that of Ruth. Ruth does not opt for a separation but for a union with Naomi until death, whereas Lot opts for a separation from Abraham during their lifetimes. Ruth makes an unconditional choice for Naomi's people and God and for Naomi herself. At no moment does she consider a separation.

Ruth is a Moabite woman and thus a descendant of Moab. Lot is the father of Moab and thus at the same time Ruth's fore-father. When this Moabite woman is married to Boaz at the end of the book, she gets a husband of quite a different descent. Boaz is in the line of Perez, the son of Judah. And Judah is a son of Jacob, and Jacob a son of Isaac, and Isaac a son of Abraham.

So Boaz stands in the genealogy that goes back to Abraham. Through the union of Ruth the Moabite woman with Boaz the man of Judah, and through the birth of Obed, the lines of Lot and Abraham come together again for the first time. Therefore a new redeemer is born with Obed, since he redeems the previous history of the clan of Abraham.

In the network of connections that the narrator makes between Ruth and Genesis we look back on the history of a people. This people was one until Abraham and his son/nephew/brother Lot separated (Gen. 13) and until several peoples formed with the birth of Moab (and Ammon) (Gen. 19). Through Boaz and Ruth and their child Obed the old and sorry break between the families of Lot and Abraham is restored. Obed redeems the history of the long-standing division and restores its unity. Thus Obed paves the way for David, the king of all Israel.

Hebrew would not be Hebrew if it did not make this reunion visible by a verbal image. The name Moab, *mo'ab*, literally means 'going out from the father'. In Genesis 19.30–38 this name indicates that the child Moab has sprung from Lot, the father of his mother. In relation to Ruth, however, the word *mo'ab* gets a wider significance. Originally Abraham and Lot belong to one people, since they come from one (grand)father. Their descendants, Israel and Moab, are thus also children of one father and therefore one people, who have gone divergent ways as a result of the separation of Lot and Abraham. As a Moabite, someone from the people of Lot, Ruth for the first time falls in with a woman of Judah. She opts for her people and for her God, and in so doing creates the conditions of the return of the Moabite people to the people of Judah (and thus of Abraham). Both through her connection with Naomi and their gradual fusion into one mother, and through her union with Boaz, there is an end to the split in the people which originally comes from one father. These people now return as it were to the one root, and from now on they can begin one common history. So Ruth, Naomi and Boaz are really the alternative ancestors of Israel and the worthy ancestors of David.

The God of Abraham and Ruth
GoGoGod

Many people have a positive picture of God: God is someone who reinforces us, who gives us the ground of our being, who intends the best for us and creates harmony in his creation. But from Genesis and Ruth it proves that God also has other faces.

In Genesis 12.1 God summons Abraham: 'Go from your country and your kindred and your father's house to the land that I will show you.' This is a very hazy summons; Abraham doesn't yet know where he has to go. He is given the promise of much land and many children, but he doesn't get this land during his lifetime; only the tiny plot of land that he buys for his wife's grave. As we read it and experience it from Abraham's perspective, God's command is not easy. Abraham has to go, and he does go, but all his life he remains 'on the go', a 'transient'. That is in fact the meaning of the word 'Hebrew' or *'ivri*. The word comes from the root *'avar*, which means pass or go through. Abraham is the traveller who always remains a foreigner, because he never lives on his own land. And Abraham is childless, since he is already ninety-nine and his wife is ninety, and they still have no children. They want to believe in God's promises, but they have to laugh when for the third time God promises that they will have a child. And God says, 'Laugh, but you'll see.' And Sarah becomes pregnant and bears a son, who is called Isaac, 'Laugh'. They laugh again, but now for joy.

The God of Abraham proves to be a God who is not always intent on harmony and stability. This God appears again in Genesis 22. 'Go,' God says to Abraham, 'Go and take your son with you and sacrifice him to me.' And wonder of wonders, Abraham goes. Crazy, one wants to say. You've waited all your life for a child and then you're ready to sacrifice him. Perhaps he has such trust in this God who continually keeps breaking into his personal life that he thinks, 'I'll wait and all will turn out well.' Just like the first time, things don't seem to go well. The turning point comes at the moment when despair is on top and Abraham has lost heart. That is true both the first time, when Abraham and Sarah get their first (and last) child, and now, when Abraham sacrifices his son. He already has the knife in his hand. A more painful picture is almost impossible to envisage: a father who is about to cut the throat of his only son. Is that the God of love? This God is not a God who makes you feel comfortable, but one who makes you feel uncomfortable. He is a God who, the moment that you have taken a great deal of trouble to get some order and structure into your life, makes you feel the chaos underneath. He is a God who breaks opens your life in a painful way the very moment that you had it firmly in your hands. He is a God who keeps telling you to get going, a GoGoGod.

Now and then God breaks into Abraham's life. And Abraham time and again lets God descend on him and does what he is told. 'Go,' and he goes. 'Circumcise,' and he circumcises. 'Sacrifice,' and he sacrifices. This Abraham is a fantastic man. Only we don't come across God so often in our daily life. We think that God never breaks in on us. We aren't called to settle abroad. We aren't called to sacrifice our child. (Of course we would never be so crazy as to obey.) So we can't show how good we are (or are not), or what good believers we are (or are not). But perhaps God broke into your life yesterday and you didn't happen to notice. Possibly he will call you to go the day after tomorrow and then you will have an eye or an ear for him.

God who breaks in

Just imagine that now, in 1997, you're carrying out a survey and ask people in the street, 'What do you live for?' and many people answer 'to be happy'. In New Age thinking this ideal is expressed in terms of 'being completely yourself' or 'finding God in yourself'. In the hedonistic or materialistic thought which is propagated above all among young people with the phrase, 'You're young and you want something', personal happiness is also central: you want excitement and sensations, love and happiness, pleasure and prosperity, health and healthy children.

The God of Abraham and the God of Ruth stands over against this. Just imagine that Ruth had sought her happiness in herself. In that case she would never have gone away with Naomi; she would never have abandoned her fatherland and her home for an uncertain future. For Ruth, the meaning of life does not lie in herself, either in personal happiness or in her becoming herself; but she wants to make Naomi and her past husband live on in an appropriate way. Moreover she opts for YHWH, Naomi's God, and allows this God to break into her Moabite order, into her safe home and the fixed system of rules. She expressly opts for this YHWH, whose very name indicates that he is a God of movement. For the word YHWH is a form of the verb to be, *haya*; to be precise it is the third person masculine singular of 'to be', i.e. 'he is'. But because the form at the same time indicates an action which is not yet complete but is continuing, you can translate YHWH as 'he is going on', 'he will be' or 'he becomes continuous'. In Exodus 3.13–14 this name is interpreted as follows:

3.13   Moses said to God,
    'If I come to the people of Israel,
    and say to them,
      "The God of your fathers has sent me to you,"
    and they ask me,
      "What is his name?"
    what shall I say to them?'
3.14   God said to Moses:
    'I am who I am.'
    And he said,
    'Say this to the people of Israel,
      "I am has sent me to you."'

YHWH explains his name as a form of the verb 'to be', but because he himself is speaking, he puts it in the first person singular. Unlike the English form, this 'being' is not definitive or complete, but still active, and therefore it is better to translate Exodus 3.14 as 'I am who I am becoming' or 'I am becoming who I am'. YHWH is then the 'God who always becomes more who he is', a dynamic God who always becomes more who he is. This YHWH keeps calling people to get moving and go on the way and thus to become who they are.

    YHWH is not a comfortable God, but a God who challenges. YHWH calls people not to remain stuck in themselves but to risk themselves. That is difficult, even painful, since most people are intent on their own preservation and their own order. Not only their actions but even their perceptions are directed towards getting a grip on the world around them: they (and we) cast a net over something and think that they can catch everything in it. Other people perceive things differently, have different lives, different cultures and principles of ordering, and thus cast other nets over reality. They feel, experience and think differently. And yet at the same time we human beings have the capacity to allow ourselves to be broken open, to let other people into our lives. Thus 'revelation' is a form of God's breaking into human life. God is the one who breaks in.

In the (post)modern period in which we live, we are becoming increasingly aware that we are all tied to our own perspective. We recognize that almost everything is determined by the person who looks or perceives, that everything depends on the time and context in which something is said, and that we cannot detach ourselves from ourselves. But this sense can be the beginning of a relativization of our own perspective and the possibility of changing our perspective. Despite the way in which we are tied to our perceptions we are in a position to allow ourselves to be broken open by someone who thinks and feels quite differently. Events which affect us and people who look at us therefore confront us most with our selves and can therefore break open the way in which we look. God, too, is such a foreigner, and God can even be a Moabite widow.

The book that you are now holding has shown you perspective after perspective and allowed you to feel what it's like to look through the eyes of other individuals. Its aim has been to break open the way in which you look at things and invite you to go on the way. So it is time now for us, too, to go.

A Guide to Reading

In this guide to reading I shall try to show you how to study a (biblical) text systematically and methodically by yourself. The guide can be applied both to the Hebrew text and the English translation, though here I shall use examples only from the English translation.

To profit as much as possible from the exercise, it's best to make a copy of a biblical translation, preferably the Revised Standard Version, which is the most literal. It is useful if you enlarge the text on a photocopier; or if you have a typewriter or word processor, you can type out the text you want to study and work with that.

Stage 1: Distinguishing between actions and speech

1. A first thing to do at this stage takes you back to nursery school: you have to cut and paste. Take an enlarged copy of the biblical text or type out a sentence from the biblical translation, giving a line to each sentence unit. A sentence unit is the shortest possible sentence which consists of a subject and a statement. If the subject or what is said (verb) changes, a new sentence unit begins, and this needs to be put on a new line. Thus you will have to cut the text 'he came, saw and conquered' into three pieces and put them one under another:

he came
(he) saw,
(he) conquered.

In short, there is one sentence unit or clause per line. Take, for example, Ruth 1.18a: 'She saw that she was resolved.' This sentence contains clauses; moreover there is a change of subject: the first 'she' is Naomi and the second 'she' is Ruth:

She saw
that she was resolved.

In the translation of Ruth placed at the beginning of each chapter the sentence units have already been distinguished. It makes sense first to try it for yourself, and then to check by 'my' Ruth whether you are right, and also whether you think that I have done it right.

2. Then you need to make a distinction between action and speech or, better, between what is done and what is spoken (for speaking is itself also an action). An action is a verb form which indicates an activity: 'he hung', 'she undertook', 'she said', 'you thought', and so on. The speech is what follows a verb denoting speaking, or after a comma, and is therefore put in inverted commas. For example:

1.11   (Naomi said):
        'Go back, my daughters.'

You can bring out this distinction in the version of the biblical text which you've made, by cutting or typing, by putting the verb right against the margin and then placing what is said a couple of centimetres inside the margin. Then you get all the actions underneath each other at the margin, and all that is said indented underneath each other. Sometimes there can be further speech within speech (She said, 'He said, "Do not come with empty hands."'). In such a case you indent the second saying two more centimetres. This has also been done in the translation of Ruth at the head of each chapter, so you will find a model there.

3. A third part within this stage is to look at the gender and number (singular or plural) of the verbs: 'you go', and 'you return'. This could be two different 'you's', one singular and one plural. For example, in Ruth 1.15 we have 'she said'. Who is this she? The last person to be spoken of in 1.14 was Ruth. But from the content of what is said, Naomi seems to be

speaking. Evidently the narrator finds it so obvious that he doesn't indicate the change of subject by a name.

In this way it becomes clear who is speaking in the book of Ruth and how much. It transpires that around 65% of the book consists of monologues or dialogues, and only 35% of narrative texts. A good deal is spoken in most biblical texts, but not as much as in Ruth. So from this first step you can draw the conclusion that Ruth is a dialogue that has got out of hand. Or, better, the book of Ruth is very like a film scenario or the script of a play. You could perform it as it is. That also explains why the book is so lively.

Stage 2: Becoming aware of who is speaking and through whose eyes we are looking

The second stage in reading is to investigate who is speaking. We have to decide whether it is (I) the narrator or (II) a character. If a character is not speaking, it must be the narrator.

I. If the narrator is speaking, then there are two possibilities.
 1. The narrator is addressing the speaker directly, as in Ruth 4.7.

4.7 This was formerly the custom in Israel in redeeming and exchanging:
  to confirm a matter
  a man took off his sandal
  and gave it to the other man.

This direct form of speech on the part of the narrator is usually called a 'commentary sentence' [A]. For example, in the sentence which you are now reading, I, the narrator, am addressing you, the readers, directly. So this is a commentary sentence. In Ruth there are very few verses direct from the narrator, or commentary sentences; they only appear in 4.7 and 4.18–22. In the Gospels we find them much more often, as for example when the evangelist says: 'Jesus did this to show his disciples that . . .'
 2. The second possibility is that the narrator does not address the reader directly but is in fact speaking. Then this is an

ordinary 'narrative text': 'It happened in the time of the judges that . . .'; 'she went away and said, ". . .".' This variant is very important and occurs by far the most frequently. These are the actions which in stage 1 are put right against the margin. Whereas at stage 1 the question was whether or not there was any action, in stage 2 the central question is who is relating these actions.

Within the narrator's text or the narrative sentence two variants occur, though the narrator is always the one who speaks. In the first, he indicates his own perspective, in which case this is a 'direct narrative sentence' [B]. In the second, he speaks from the perspective of a character: this is an 'indirect narrative sentence' [C]. So in the book of Ruth the sentences

1.1   A man went away from Bethlehem in Judah
        to live as an emigrant in the country of Moab,
        he, his wife and his two sons.

1.14   She kissed them,
        they lifted up their voices
        and burst into tears.

are examples of direct narrative sentences which are to be attributed to the narrator: they are spoken and seen by the narrator. By contrast, in verbs which indicate a perception, thought, feeling or experience of a character, we have an indirect narrative sentence, for example in Ruth,

1.6   Naomi had heard
        that YHWH had visited his people to give them bread.

1.18a   She saw
        that she was resolved
        to go with her.

These verses are related by the narrator, but from Naomi's perspective. Other examples of an indirect narrative sentence are: 'She didn't feel well', 'he was aware of his defective way of speaking', 'we could just sink into the ground, we're so miserable'. You should be able to develop antennae for words like 'see', 'hear', 'think', 'feel', 'experience', 'be afraid', 'hope', in short for words which express a character's thoughts, perceptions or feelings. In other words, with a direct narrative sentence the narrator is speaking and as readers we perceive through his eyes; in an indirect narrative sentence the narrator is speaking, but we perceive through the eyes of the character.

II. The other main group is the one in which a character speaks. It is better to say that the narrator makes a character speak for himself or herself. In such a situation we speak of an 'embedded speaker's text'. In the translation I have marked these with an indentation as 'what is spoken', so that they are easy to recognize. The person who speaks always speaks from his or her own perspective, and thus presents his or her own awareness, feeling, perception, experience or conviction. What is said is thus always expressed by the character. In many forms of textual exegesis people make a mistake here: they make the narrator responsible for what a character says, or God responsible for what a character or the narrator thinks. Thus distinguishing who is speaking has far-reaching consequences.

Again there are two variants in the case of an embedded speaker's text.

1. A narrator presents what is spoken directly. The character speaks in direct speech [D]. This occurs very often in Ruth, as I have remarked:

1.16   'Where you go
       I shall go.'

2.19   'The name of the man
       with whom I worked today
       is Boaz.'

3.18   'Wait, my daughter,
       until you know
       how the matter turns out.'

As a reader, one is looking through the eyes of the character, who often speaks in the first person.

2. The other possibility is for the character to speak, but for the narrator to indicate this indirectly. This is then described as

indirect speech. A general example is: she said that she was tired (as opposed to direct speech: 'She said, "I am tired."'). This form does not occur very often in Ruth, but we do find it in 2.19:

2.19 She told her mother-in-law
with whom she had worked.

Thus in both the direct and the indirect speech the character is speaking. These are two forms of speaker's text, and only the way in which the narrator presents them differs.

3. 17a She (= Ruth) said,
'These six measures of barley he gave to me,
17b for, he said,
"You must not go back empty-handed to your mother-in-law."'

Even more deeply embedded speech is possible, like a direct speech embedded in a direct speech which is embedded in another direct speech (as in Ruth 4.4).

Finally, let me mention a good help for stage 2, namely the personal pronouns. After you've determined whether the perspective is that of the narrator or that of a character, you can use the personal pronouns to see with whom you are looking. For example, if Elimelek is called 'her husband', the perspective is that of Naomi; or if Naomi is called 'his wife', the perspective is that of Elimelek. Another example is Ruth 1.15:

1.15 She said,
'See, your sister-in-law is going back to her people and her God.'

Naomi says 'your' sister-in-law to Ruth, but not 'your' people and 'your' God. Is this God of the sister-in-law then not Ruth's God? Often personal pronouns betray something of the perspective from which someone thinks or feels.

All these positions can be summed up as follows:

I. The narrator speaks	
1 directly	= commentary sentence
2 indirectly a: from his own perspective b: from the perspective of the character	= narrative sentence = direct narrative sentence = indirect narrative sentence
II. The character speaks	
1 directly	= direct speech
2 indirectly	= indirect speech

In the form of a tree this looks like this:

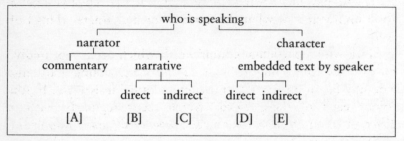

This means that in situation [A] the reader is being addressed directly and informed by the narrator. In situation [B] the reader perceives through the eyes and mouth of the narrator via the story. Situation [C] makes the reader look through the eyes of the character but in the words of the narrator. In situation [D] the reader perceives directly what a character perceives and narrates. Finally, in situation [E] the reader perceives indirectly what a character perceives and narrates.

Stage 3: Looking at lines of meaning

A third and last step is to try to trace the lines of meaning which occur in the text. You can do this through the following subdivisions.

Make a list of the words which indicate time and place. For example, in Ruth 1.1, 'In the days when the rulers gave leadership'; 1.4b ' they lived there about ten years'. Examples of place are 'Bethlehem in Judah', (1.1), 'land of Moab' (1.1, 2, 6), 'field in Moab' (1.6). And see whether you can bring in a particular line there. Then you can compare this with 'my' funnel shape, which I brought out in Chapter 3.

Make a list of the words which indicate a movement, like 'go', 'return', 'come', and try to find a line. For example, in the first half of Ruth words of movement (return, go) play an important role, but not in the second half.

Make a list of the names used for God: YHWH, the Almighty, and the like, and see who uses which names. Thus Naomi uses only the name Almighty (1.20).

You can also look to see whether the same words are always attached to God, as in Ruth : 'blessing and YHWH' (2.4,20; 3.10; 4.14) and 'gift and YHWH' (1.6, 9; 4.11, 12, 13). Then you get a good impression of what the narrator or a character thinks of God.

Mark with a particular colour words which occur repeatedly, for example 'they clung to' in 1.14 and 2.23, 'young man' and 'young woman' in Ruth 2, 'proclaim a name' in Ruth 4. If you colour each of these words which recur regularly with a different colour, you will soon get a view of the most important themes of the text.

Try to look at the connection between words or groups of connected words of one colour, e.g. mother-in-law – daughter-in-law – daughter, or man – wife – young man – young woman. You can do that by looking at the distribution in the text, by listing what is said by one word or another.

You can also investigate how something of roughly the same content is said by the different characters: this is the distribution of the use of words over the characters. Thus in Ruth Boaz and Naomi use the word 'know' and Ruth does not. This can say something about the knowledge or the world of one character as opposed to another.

In the end, you will find that you're missing a great deal because you don't have the Hebrew text in front of you and so you can't see all the word-plays or lines of language; far less can you enjoy the style and imagery of the text. Perhaps the next step is for you to learn Hebrew!

A Short Bibliography

Biblia Hebraica Stuttgartensia, Ruth (ed. T.H. Robinson), Württembergische Bibelanstalt, Stuttgart 1975

Berlin, A., 'Poetics in the Book of Ruth', *Poetics and Interpretation of Biblical Narrative*, Bible and Interpretation Series 9, The Almond Press, Sheffield 1983, 83–110

Bernstein, M.J., 'Two Multivalent Readings in the Ruth Narrative', *Journal for the Study of the Old Testament* 50, 1991, 15–26

Busch, F.W., *Ruth, Esther*, Word Bible Commentary Vol.9, Word Books, Dallas 1996

Campbell, F. F., *Ruth. A New Translation with Introduction and Commentary*, The Anchor Bible, Doubleday, Garden City, New York 1975

Davies, F.W., 'Ruth IV 5 and the Duties of the Go'el', *Vetus Testamentum* 33, 1983, 231–4

Fiseb, H., 'Ruth and the Structure of Covenant History', *Vetus Testamentum* 32, 1982, 425–37

Gow, M.D., *The Book of Ruth. Its Structure, Theme and Purpose*, Apollos 1994

Hubbard, R. L., *The Book of Ruth*, The New International Commentary on the Old Testament, Eerdmans, Grand Rapids, Michigan 1988

Labuschagne, C.J., 'The Crux in Ruth 4,11', *Zeitschrift für die alttestamentliche Wissenschaft* 79, 1967, 364–7

Niditch, S., 'Legends of Heroes and Heroines', in *The Hebrew Bible and its Modern Interpreters*, ed. D.A. Knight and G.M.Tucker, Scholars Press, Chico, California 1985, 451–6

Nielsen, K., 'Le choix contre le droit dans le livre de Ruth. De l'aire de battage au tribunal', *Vetus Testamentum* 35, 1985, 201–12

—, *Ruth. A Commentary*, Louisville, Westminster John Knox Press and London, SCM Press 1997

Porten, B., 'The Scroll of Ruth: A Rhetorical Study', *Gratz College Annual of Jewish Studies* 7, 1978, 23–49

Prinsloo, W.S., 'The Theology of the Book of Ruth', *Vetus Testamentum* 30, 1980, 330–41

Rauber, D.F., 'Literary Values in the Bible. The Book of Ruth', *Journal of Biblical Literature* 89, 1970, 27–37

Sasson, J.M., *Ruth. A New Translation with a Philological Commentary and a Formalist-Folklorist Interpretation*, The Johns Hopkins University Press, Baltimore and London 1979

Theissen, G., 'Seduction to Life. A Woman's Story from a Male Perspective (The Book of Ruth)', in *Traces of Light. Sermons and Bible Studies*, SCM Press, London 1996, 47–62